JOHN BROWN EN(
Power Contractors

John Hood

© John Hood 2004

Published by Aker Kværner.
Printed by J&J Robertson, Dumbarton, Scotland.

Disclaimer
In writing this history, I have drawn upon a number of sources, including company Report & Accounts, company newsletters and brochures, and newspaper articles, etc. I have also been privileged to have had the opportunity to speak with a number of people who were employed by, or involved with, JBE over the years. Whilst I have made every effort to verify the facts, I am inevitably reliant on their perceptions and interpretation of past events. I am most grateful to all of those whom I interviewed, for giving of their time and assistance to the project. I have attempted to do them the courtesy of recording accurately their recollections and opinions. For the avoidance of doubt, I should however make clear that the views and opinions expressed in the book do not necessarily reflect those of the author or of Aker Kvaerner.

John Hood
February 2004

ISBN 0-9547453-0-2

Contents   Page No.

Acknowledgements

Prologue

1	**Introduction**	**9**
2	**The Birth of John Brown Engineering**	**14**
	The Decision to separate the Engine Works from the Shipyard	14
	JBE: Structure, Personnel and Site Boundaries	15
3	**Marine Engines and Gas Turbines: JBE seeks its markets**	**20**
	Marine Engine Work	20
	The move into Gas Turbine Manufacture	22
4	**The Development of Gas Turbine Work**	**29**
	Manufacturing for Clients other than GE	29
	Packaged Power Plants: JBE takes another step forward	35
	JBE: the progress so far ...	38
5	**Oil: A Window of Opportunity**	**40**
	Oil Pipeline Turbines	40
	Turbines for the North Sea	43
	A Foray into Fabrication: the story of JBE Offshore Limited	44
6	**JBE: The Company in the late 1970s**	**50**
	Setting up JBE Gas Turbines Limited	50
	Looking back on JBE's first ten years	50
	... and looking to the present	52
	Tough Times	55
7	**Three Projects memorable for the wrong reasons**	**62**
	Bani Yas	62
	Iraq	63
	JBE and the Russian Pipeline Embargo	65

8	**Back from the Brink**	**68**
	The Hawker Siddeley Take-over Bid	68
	A New Team	69
	The Men and the Management	70
	Attempts to strengthen JBE	71
	Water and Sewerage: a new opportunity	74
9	**JBE in Trafalgar House**	**76**
	Trafalgar House steps in	76
	The Projects	78
	Structural Changes	85
	Keadby	89
	The post-Keadby Era	91
10	**The Kvaerner Era**	**93**
	Kvaerner takes over at the Helm	93
	Business as usual	95
	KEL goes Up for Sale	97
	The Beginning of the End	99
11	**Conclusion**	**103**

Milestones for John Brown Engineering	106
List of Gas Turbine contracts undertaken by JBE	107
Bibliography and References	113

Acknowledgements

Much assistance and encouragement has been received from many individuals in the preparation of this book. While it is impossible to acknowledge everyone by name, I should like to thank in particular: Gavin Barrie, Donald Beveridge, Tony Bird, Ian Broadley, Andy Clark, Joe Craig, Dick Cummings, Stuart Currie, Donnie Ferguson, Jack Findlay, Alan Forbes, Allan Gormly, Willie Grant, Nigel Hill, Bob Hepburn, John Innes, Willie Ireland, Bill Law, Jim Liddell, Jim McDowell, Donald MacLeod, David Mitchell, Alan Ottley, Mike Pell, Tom Rae, Robbie Robertson, John Thomson, Ron Tosh and Alan Young (all former John Brown Engineering employees); and Andrew Capps, Ian Deans, David Farquharson, Ian Gillies, Hugh McGinty and Jim Swan (all previously JBE, now GE). I should also like to thank Mrs. Joan Connell, Mrs. Catherine Strachan, John Durber (formerly Managing Director of Brush Electrical Engineering Limited), and Sid Gait and John Fitzsimons (both formerly of John Brown Land Boilers Limited). Thanks are also due to Ian Watson (Picture Librarian, *The Herald*); Lesley Richmond and George Gardner (both Glasgow University Archives); and Pat Malcolm (West Dunbartonshire Libraries) for assistance with photographs.

Particular thanks are due to: Chris Packard (formerly President, Kvaerner Energy Limited), who first had the idea of writing the history of JBE, for his constant patience, support and encouragement in the preparation of this manuscript; and Raymond McCabe (formerly Managing Director, JBE), Alaister Forsyth (formerly Operations Director, JBE) and Alex Crawford (formerly Executive Vice-President, Power Projects, KEN) for their unfailing kindness and patience in allowing me to interview them, and in assisting with the many enquiries that arose during the preparation of the manuscript. Above all, I am most grateful to my wife and daughter for their unstinting support throughout this project.

John Hood
February 2004

Prologue

In the heady days of 1993 and 1994, over twenty-five years after John Brown had retired from building ships and started in the energy business with gas turbines designed by General Electric of the USA, business was very strong. Records of employment, workload, turnover and profit, were being set with regularity and the Company won its 6th Queens Award for Export Achievement (a national record at that time). Just six years later, the days of John Brown (then under Kvaerner at Clydebank) had ended, but the bonds of friendship which had kept so many of the people who worked for the Company together, still remain. The pride and passion of all the people who worked for the Company was intense and is no better exemplified than when I was introduced to a fitter working for Aramco in Saudi Arabia. His supervisor told me that the fitter had worked for John Brown and that was the reason he had given him a job. I was surprised that I didn't know the gentleman, who eventually confessed that he had actually only worked for the Company for one week - ten years earlier!

It was the very success of 1993 - 1994 that proved the Company's undoing. The quality of its engineering and workmanship continued in the traditional vein that saw the world's greatest liners launched from the Clydebank yard, but the cost of this quality and the volume of work was greater than the superhuman efforts of so many could manage. In 1995, principally the cost of quality and the earlier difficulty in attracting enough skilled engineers to the business, conspired to cause the Company to crash badly from its exalted position. So great was the crash that it took all of the next six years to sweep up the debris.

Despite these problems, which contributed in no small way to the takeover of John Brown's parent company, Trafalgar House, the arrival of Kvaerner was viewed by many at Clydebank as that of a white knight who had come to our rescue, and indeed for a number of years this appeared to be the case.

When Erik Tonseth, the CEO of Kvaerner, left and GE's licence conditions under which the Company manufactured its gas turbines became more onerous, the future started to look very bleak again. As Kvaerner was forced to rein back, inevitably the highly successful Services arm of the Company was targeted for sale, and eventually both it and the Power Projects Division were sold to GE. Whilst attempts were made to try to sell the remaining Clydebank factory as a working unit with an expectation of a satisfactory workload from GE, none of the potential buyers was able to agree terms adequate to safeguard its future, despite the support of the Scottish Executive. The underlying reason that prevented such a sale was almost certainly the fear of the unknown - after 160 years of working on the site, how badly was the land polluted, and who would take the responsibility for cleaning it up?

Despite its financial difficulties, and with closure of the factory becoming inevitable, Kvaerner agreed a package of compensation for all the remaining workforce. At the end of March 2001, some thirty-five years after the cessation of Shipbuilding and the start of the Gas Turbine business, the machinery stopped turning, the welders stopped welding, and the factory fell silent. It was of enormous credit to the workforce, both management and Unions, that every last order was completed to quality and ahead of schedule.

It is now nearly three years since this final chapter in the colourful life of the Company ended, and it is only with the benefit of hindsight that one can look back and surmise what might have happened had the factory been sold as a going concern. It was not long after the closure that the stream of orders for new gas turbines dramatically collapsed and, unless much had changed, the work would have dried up and the factory threatened with closure yet again. It is unlikely that the severance terms that would have been available from a new management would have been anything like as benign as those agreed by Kvaerner. There is now little doubt that the inevitable end of arguably the world's most famous shipyard of the twentieth century was, under Kvaerner, the most dignified option for all those men and women who were privileged to have worked there.

With such a colourful history, of which much has already been recorded, particularly about the days of shipbuilding, the final chapter had to be written. Before the factory closed, I asked John Hood if he would write his account of John Brown Engineering and Kvaerner Energy as makers of Gas Turbines and builders of Power Stations over the last thirty-five years. This is it.

Chris Packard
Formerly Managing Director of John Brown Engineering, and
President of Kvaerner Energy Limited.

February 2004

1   Introduction

The Engine Works of John Brown & Company (Clydebank) Limited were perhaps an unseen, but certainly vital, part of this Shipyard's successes. From 1884 until the late 1940s, the Engine Works was primarily engaged in the manufacture of a range of marine engines and other machinery for ships built in the Yard. Initially the marine engines manufactured were mostly reaction steam turbine engines of the type patented in 1884 by Charles Algernon Parsons, however, later the Engine Works also manufactured Curtis impulse steam turbines. These turbines, first patented in 1896 by the American Charles Gordon Curtis, were further developed by him in collaboration with the General Electric Company (GE) at their Schenectady plant in New York. Ironically, given the strong link that would later evolve between John Brown Engineering Limited (JBE) and GE, Curtis' turbine was further developed under licence in Clydebank in 1903 by Thomas (later Sir Thomas) Bell, the then Managing Director of John Brown & Company (Clydebank) Limited. To oversee this work, GE's Stephen Pigott was recruited in 1908. The latter worked on an experimental turbine set that was erected at Clydebank which, after exhaustive testing and design improvements, resulted in the manufacture of the Brown-Curtis turbine at Clydebank. This turbine rivalled the Parsons steam turbine model and was used in many Clydebank-built ships. Steam turbine manufacture continued into the late 1960s, and the Engine Works also began to build (again under licence) a range of marine diesel engines of the Sulzer and Doxford type.

The steam drum for a JBLB land boiler, in front of the Engine Works

By 1945, however, the scarcity of marine engine orders forced John Brown & Company (Clydebank) Limited to diversify into other areas to supplement the work on the few marine engines then under construction. One such major diversification was the manufacture of land boilers for power stations. This was in addition to the manufacture of marine boilers carried out in the Boiler Works at the west end of the Yard. This diversification was authorised by the parent company in 1950 and was, until 1954, undertaken by a new division of John Brown & Company (Clydebank) Limited. This operation was independent of the Engine Works and was carried out at Whitecrook on a site leased from Scottish Industrial Estates Limited. From 1952 land boilers were manufactured under licence from Riley Stoker Corporation of America. The division was elevated in 1954 to the status of a wholly-owned subsidiary: John Brown Land Boilers Limited (JBLB). In 1961 JBLB merged with Foster Wheeler of America to form a new company, Foster Wheeler John Brown Limited. By 1964, with the Whitecrook Works unable to handle the volume of work, the company moved down river to occupy the former Denny shipyard in Dumbarton.

A Francis water turbine for a NOSHEB project, under construction in the Engine Works Bay 10

Another major, but temporary, diversification carried out from 1948 to 1965, was the manufacture of Kaplan, Pelton and Francis water turbines in Bay 10 of the Engine Works. These were manufactured under licence from Boving & Company Limited, London, and (with the exception of an installation at Owen Falls, Uganda) were principally for the newly nationalised North of Scotland Hydro-Electric Board (NOSHEB). Among the NOSHEB hydro-electric power stations supplied with Clydebank-built water turbines were Cluny, Cruachan, Grudie Bridge, Quoich, Strathfarrar and Torr Achilty. Of particular note was the contract awarded in 1959 by NOSHEB for their showpiece pumped storage installation at Cruachan: two Francis water turbines built by John Brown & Company (Clydebank) Limited drove the world's first high head reversible pumped storage station. The water turbines were designed to also work in reverse, thus enabling the Station to pump water back up to the high reservoir for re-use as required. The last Clydebank-built water turbine supplied to NOSHEB was installed in 1965 in the Killin Hydro-Electric Power Station.

In addition to their water turbine work, the Engine Works undertook miscellaneous 'one-off' projects, such as the construction and installation of an experimental wind generator at Costa Head in the Orkney Islands. This was said to be the first large-scale windmill project in the UK and was intended to provide electricity to the national grid. The contract, placed with Clydebank by NOSHEB in 1949, reflected the latter's interest in utilising wind power to supplement more traditional sources of electricity. A wholly steel construction, the 78 feet windmill (complete with gear box and generator) was shipped out to the Orkney Islands in late 1950. However, due to severe weather conditions, it was not erected until the spring of 1951! Ultimately, after five years of testing, NOSHEB concluded that the windmill's erratic output rendered it uneconomical, and accordingly this experimental work was terminated in 1956. The windmill was dismantled.

A further and later diversification in the mid to late 1960s was the fabrication of legs for the oil rig platforms which were being built in the old John Brown[i] shipyard by Upper Clyde Shipbuilders (Clydebank Division). By 1969, with the completion of a set of legs (each 355 feet long and weighing 600 tons) for the oil platform, *Offshore Mercury*, JBE could rightly claim to be among the world leaders in this specialist field.

Undoubtedly, however, the most significant diversification from the late 1940s onwards came from the experimental work carried out at Clydebank (and elsewhere in the UK) on open and closed cycle gas turbines for electricity generation and marine applications. Much of this experimental work was financed by government departments or agencies such as NOSHEB and was designed to provide an alternative to the more traditional steam and diesel engines. In Clydebank a Gas Turbine Department was set up as a separate section within the Engine Works. The overall responsibility for the experimental work fell to the Engine Works Manager, George Strachan, but the day-to-day running of the Department was the responsibility, firstly, of a Swiss engineer, J.D.M. Bucher, and later, JBE employee John Campbell Murray. One of John's staff at that time was Bill Connell, who was destined to play a major and key role in JBE in later years. Bill was a Glasgow man who, after graduating from the University of Glasgow with a First Class Honours degree, worked in the Ministry of Defence torpedo factory at Greenock and later with Rolls Royce. Having joined John Brown & Company (Clydebank) Limited in the 1950s to assist in the developmental work of the Gas Turbine Department, he progressed through the Department, and eventually became its Head.

The experimental gas turbine work at Clydebank started in 1948 on a small 500hp Pametrada-designed open cycle gas turbine, which had been constructed at Clydebank. This turbine was later converted into a closed cycle gas turbine with the addition of an air heater.

Simultaneously, the Department took out a licence with Escher Wyss of Switzerland to enable them to market and sell their closed cycle gas turbine. During the Department's brief lifetime several firm orders were secured for the Escher Wyss closed cycle gas turbine, including two in 1948 (from NOSHEB and the West Midlands Gas Board). The NOSHEB order was for the first UK commercial closed cycle gas turbine - a 12.5mw gas turbine for installation in Carolina Port Power Station in Dundee, designed to run on heavy oil. The West Midlands Gas Board order was for a 7mw gas turbine for the Foleshill Gas Works in Coventry, and was designed to run on waste heat. A third Escher Wyss gas turbine was installed in the mid-1950s in the National Coal Board's new showpiece Rothes Colliery at Glenrothes. Unlike the Dundee and Coventry turbines, this one used coal slurry as a fuel. Unfortunately, this turbine was never allowed to prove itself, because major geological problems forced the closure of this colliery.

By far the most important aspect of the gas turbine experimental work in the Engine Works, however, was the work carried out for NOSHEB (the project funders) and the Scottish Peat Committee, throughout the late 1940s and early 1950s. The aim of this was to design a modified 2mw Escher Wyss gas turbine capable of running on processed peat. By successfully undertaking such significant new experimental work, John Brown & Company (Clydebank) Limited Chairman, Lord Aberconway, was confident the company would become "leaders not followers"[ii] in this field. The work on the experimental gas turbine was inspected in late December 1951 by members of the Scottish Peat Committee (including Sir Edward Appleton, Chairman) and T. Lawrie (General Manager of NOSHEB). At that time Managing Director, Dr. James McNeill, indicated that tests showed the gas turbine was operating adequately, and that work was progressing satisfactorily on a tubular air heater accessory required to dry out the milled pulverised peat. By October 1952, all tests were completed, and NOSHEB felt confident enough to proceed with their proposed £1m scheme to construct a peat burning plant on a 60 acre site at Braehour Farm on Altnabreac Moss in

The NOSHEB peat burning plant at remote Altnabreac

Caithness. Site work began in 1954 and, in that same year, NOSHEB agreed a £428,967 contract with the Clydebank company for the supply of the gas turbine plant. Although it had been agreed that the plant would be operational by February 1957, vibration problems in the alternator meant that the plant was not finally commissioned until August 1959.

Ultimately, the results of the experimental work on the closed cycle gas turbine used by Clydebank, and others, demonstrated that the turbines, while capable of functioning reasonably efficiently, were not commercially viable at that time. For example, the cost of generating electricity at Dundee using the Escher Wyss turbine was three-and-a-half times more than the use of hydro-electricity. This fact, together with problems in the compressor blade mechanism, resulted in the turbine being removed in 1958 and all monies returned to NOSHEB. Similar problems were encountered at Altnabreac. While this plant was finally accepted by NOSHEB, deficiencies in the design of the air heater resulted in the clients withholding 20 per cent of the agreed contract price. In 1962, recognising that even if further expenditure was authorised to remedy these design faults the cost of the electricity produced would compare unfavourably with existing schemes, NOSHEB abandoned this experiment.

The likelihood of poor financial returns, coupled with the failure of the Dundee and Altnabreac turbines, made John Brown & Company (Clydebank) Limited form the opinion that the gas turbine field was at that time too much of a high risk undertaking. Therefore, in the early 1960s the Gas Turbine Department was closed down and Bill Connell (amongst others) left the company. This was not, however, to be the end of the association between gas turbines and the John Brown name: rather it was only the beginning.

---

i   This shipyard was owned by John Brown & Company Limited from 1899 until 1967, when it became part of Upper Clyde Shipbuilders.
ii *Clydebank Press* (1951), 28 December, p4.

2 The Birth of John Brown Engineering

The Decision to separate the Engine Works from the Shipyard

Throughout the early to mid-1960s, and despite further attempts by the company to diversify from their traditional marine engineering operations into more profitable areas of activity, both the Shipyard and the Engine Works at Clydebank continued to be a financial drain on the parent company's resources. In the financial year ending 31 March 1966, for example, Lord Aberconway reported Group losses of £2.2m, despite a reasonable overall performance and some mixed results in the Machine Tools and General Engineering Divisions. He noted particularly the anticipated £3m loss on the Clydebank-built *MV Kungsholm* contract (which he called "the most disastrous financially, that Clydebank has ever executed"[i]) and the anticipated loss by sister company, Constructors John Brown (CJB), who were at that point losing money on Algerian pipeline contracts. The Engine Works at Clydebank was also experiencing financial problems, and with fixed overheads more than double the amount recoverable on contracts taken, rumours were circulating regarding its possible closure. Understandably this created anxiety at all levels in Clydebank and led the Engine Works Director, George Strachan, to prepare a case against closure. This he presented to parent company Board members, Tom Burleigh and John Staniforth, demonstrating that the Engine Works did not generally lose money. Although the *QE2*, *MV Kungsholm* and *HMS Intrepid* contracts had proved so disastrous for the shipyard side of the business, the Engine Works had in fact made a profit on their part of the contracts. Whether Strachan's intervention influenced the parent company is unclear, but the decision was ultimately made in 1965 to separate the Engine Works from the Shipyard, and transfer the Engine Works' assets to a new wholly-owned subsidiary company.

In doing so, John Brown & Company anticipated one of the principal recommendations of the Shipbuilding Inquiry Committee (commonly known as the Geddes Committee) set up in February 1965 by the then recently elected Labour Prime Minister, Harold Wilson, to report on the perceived over-capacity within the UK shipbuilding and marine engineering industries. The Committee, under the chairmanship of (later Sir) Reay M. Geddes OBE, was at the outset conscious that the UK's share of the world market had plunged from 50 per cent in 1950 to a low of under 10 per cent in 1965, although they were optimistic that this trend could be reversed with extra resources. However, of all the recommendations made in the resultant *Geddes Report*,[ii] published in March 1966, the two which most affected Clydebank were: the proposed merger of five Clydeside yards to create a new grouping to be known as Upper Clyde Shipbuilders Limited (UCS), and the separation of the Engine Works from the Shipyards. The Committee recommended the latter as a measure to tackle the decline in engine production within the UK industry: in the ten years from 1956 to 1965, it had fallen from 825,900 hp to 569,400 hp. The Committee also argued that the realistically available work could easily be carried out by reducing the number of existing engine manufacturers throughout the UK to four, broadly matching their proposal that the number of existing UK shipyards be reduced by forming no more than five major groupings on roughly geographical lines. In respect of the several UK engine manufacturers, the Committee anticipated the likely demand for the increasingly popular diesel engines, such as Sulzer's, which were more compact and had (apart from the advantages in power and speed) lower running costs in comparison with more traditional steam turbines. The recommendation to separate Engine Works from the Shipyards, and the subsequent promise of grants and loans from the proposed Shipbuilding Industry Board to be set up in the wake of the *Geddes Report*, undoubtedly convinced the parent company that their earlier decision to separate had been correct. The parent company's initiative - they were the first UK shipbuilder (and only one of two shipbuilders on the Clyde) to adopt this particular recommendation - was undoubtedly a landmark decision.

Once the Board had begun to action its decision to separate the Engine Works from the Shipyard, a name for the new company had to be found. Initially, the Clydebank management simply proposed John Brown Engineering, but this was rejected by the London Board in favour of 'Clydebank Engineering'. Once again George Strachan intervened, and the resulting version - John Brown Engineering (Clydebank) Limited - was most likely something of a compromise between Clydebank and London. On 16 September 1966 this name was confirmed by a company resolution, and on 1 October the new wholly-owned subsidiary officially came into existence. Although it still shared its site with the Shipyard, it was in every other respect a separate company from the latter, which traded from 1967 until 1968 as John Brown Shipbuilders Limited, and then as the Clydebank Division of the newly-created UCS.

JBE: Structure, Personnel and Site Boundaries

To all intents and purposes the separation of the Engine Works from the Shipyard was painless, with most existing staff and workers transferring from the Engine Works on the Friday and reporting to JBE on the following Monday. However, as the Director and General Manager of the new company, Graham Strachan, commented in its first *Newsletter*,[iii] although many things appeared the same, the separation necessitated changes in, for example, the financial set up of the two companies.

Until the early 1970s subsidiaries like JBE would be afforded a large measure of local autonomy, provided the parent company was kept informed. For example, JBE had its own Board of Directors with Sir George Gardner (a Board member of the parent company in London) as its Chairman. The former Engine Works Manager and Deputy Managing Director of John Brown's Clydebank Shipyard, George Strachan, was briefly Deputy Chairman. His son, Graham Robert Strachan, was Director and General Manager. While George Strachan was nominally in charge of the Clydebank company, his was largely an interim appointment to enable the new company to establish itself, and it was his son, Graham, who would ultimately bear the responsibility of guiding JBE through its early formative years. Although basically shy and retiring, Graham Strachan was willing and happy to lead from the front in his dealings with industry and the media. He was seen by the parent company as the acceptable face of JBE, and was, crucially, particularly skilful in choosing the right people for the job, as well as shrewd enough to give them their head and allow them (albeit under his direction) to fully develop the new business. On his father's retirement in 1969 Graham became Managing Director - a position he would fill with distinction for many years.

Among the other key personnel who transferred to JBE from the Engine Works was the former Financial Controller of the Shipyard, Alastair Smith. He became Secretary and

Accountant to the new Company, responsible for all secretarial, accounting and commercial activities. Other important staff members included Bill Davie who, as Engineering Manager, was responsible for all aspects of production and the operation of all the Works Departments; and Jim Turner, who was responsible for sales, estimating and tendering activities.

George Strachan, Deputy Chairman JBE 1966-69 (on the left) talks with JBE Chairman, Sir George Gardner, after the first Queens Award ceremony in 1970

In addition, Bill Connell was enticed back to Clydebank in 1965 by Graham Strachan, largely because of his previous experience as Head of the old Gas Turbine Department. He became Technical Manager,[iv] responsible for design, development and the Drawing Offices. His was a shrewd appointment, for he quickly became a valuable right-hand man to Graham Strachan. Bill had a strong personality, and was an enthusiast and extrovert, who inspired the people working under him. While he didn't suffer fools gladly, he always appreciated and admired the great team of men he worked with. Importantly, he had the vision to encourage the new company to shake off old traditional and parochial Shipyard attitudes, and adopt a more professional approach to the new business of gas turbine manufacture. Above all, he was a very good salesman and was adept in promoting and marketing JBE's image on a world-wide basis. Bill saw his primary role as winning contracts and to do so was prepared to travel far and wide. At the launch of the *QE2*, for example, Bill was in China cultivating potential clients in a market that he had high hopes of ultimately penetrating. He often accompanied GE's Regional Sales Manager, Morgan Ryan, with whom he worked closely, giving joint sales presentations in countries such as Canada and Australia, to make the name JBE known within the international gas turbine market. He was especially proud of contacts made in, for example, the United Arab Emirates, and established good working relationships with the three Masaood Brothers (JBE's local agents) in Abu Dhabi.

The positions of Boiler Works Manager and Projects Manager in the new company were filled by Joe Craig and Alaister Forsyth. The latter (who had previously worked closely with

Bill Connell in Duncan Stewart's at Glasgow) was brought to Clydebank as Bill Connell's deputy, although ultimately they divided their responsibilities: Bill dealing with pre-order issues and Alaister with post-order issues. Like Bill, Alaister brought drive and enthusiasm to the new company and his understanding of the limitations of gas turbines technology meant that he became in many ways the person people went to for expert technical advice.

Having established the senior management structure, the next requirement was to recruit the remaining workforce and this was done, in the main, by simply transferring Engine Works personnel across to the new company. Notwithstanding ingrained Union attitudes and traditional demarcation positions, the new workforce was generally enthusiastic. Although changes to working practices did require to be made, the willingness of the workers to absorb these, and new skills, undoubtedly contributed to the early success of the company. This would be particularly demonstrated with the early Russian contracts, which required far greater discipline in respect of meeting deadlines and the supply of contract items: Russian clients could (and would) reject any shipment unless the consignment was 100 per cent complete. Notwithstanding the workers' co-operation, the excessive number of Unions - and the resultant demarcation disputes - remained a problem for management until into the early 1980s. This, coupled with the problem of low productivity, was highlighted in the first company *Newsletter*. Graham Strachan stressed the need for efficiencies in order to secure, and timeously complete, orders while accruing sufficient funds both to update plant and equipment and finance the business - and make a profit for the company. One of the early necessary major initiatives was to change the old 'one-off' order mentality, whereby marine

Machinery being hoisted on board ship in the traditional way

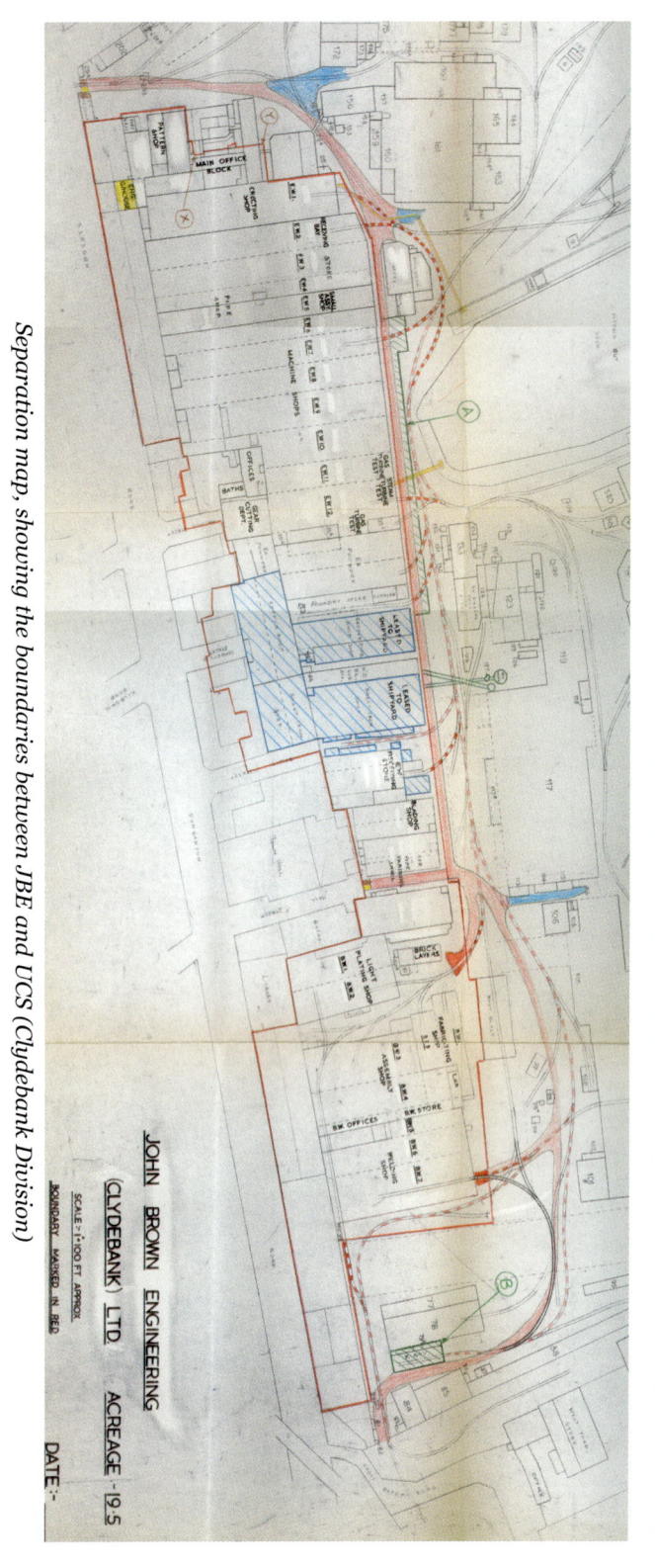

Separation map, showing the boundaries between JBE and UCS (Clydebank Division)

engines were seen as separate and single orders; in contrast the manufacture of gas turbines was more akin to continuous 'batch' processing requiring assembly line techniques. The general impression in 1966 was that JBE was organisationally very backward and very much a foreman-dominated organisation. For example, most machinery for ships built in Clydebank was manufactured in the Engine Works and then 'barrowed' across to the ships without the proper production control and planning systems one would have expected.

Notwithstanding these difficulties, the workforce responded well to the new technology. Many years of building diesel engines, and water and steam turbines, had led to the development of skills which were quickly adapted to gas turbine manufacture. As has been seen, the newly-formed Industrial Turbine Department and the new production functions had to be turned into assembly line operation rather than one-off manufacture, and progress to producing high quality, 'right-first-time' products for an increasingly competitive international market. Inevitably this took a considerable number of years. The early teething problems are demonstrated by a humorous (and oft-recounted!) anecdote concerning the first control cabin shipped to the US. Apparently when the floor plates were being painted at Clydebank,

– 18 –

two loose spanners were spray-painted in situ. When GE field personnel in the US opened up the cab and saw the two spanners, they were horrified. Clydebank's response was to ask for their spanners back - a humorous riposte which defused an embarrassing situation.

Another of the new company's first priorities was to determine its physical boundaries. Essentially, it extended from the No.1 Engine Shop to the Welding Shop, with the nucleus of the new business centred round the old, largely self-contained, 1884 Engine Works. Reputedly, George Strachan simply took a red pen to an existing site map and drew a line to separate the former Engine Works from the Shipyard. However, in reality it was not that simple. UCS (Clydebank Division) still continued to have buildings within the JBE portion, and similarly JBE had buildings within the UCS portion. In the event, the site was split into five operational areas:

1. Areas wholly owned by UCS (Clydebank Division);
2. Areas wholly owned by JBE;
3. Common areas, which included access and roadways;
4. Areas owned by UCS (Clydebank Division) but leased to JBE (these included car parks, storage areas, and canteen and ambulance facilities); and
5. Areas owned by JBE but leased to UCS (Clydebank Division) (for example, the copper and sheet iron shops).

Although the layout of the various JBE buildings greatly altered over the years, this boundary line (with a few minor exceptions) remained largely intact until the final demise of KEL in 2001.

In early 1972 after a period of lengthy consideration a decision would finally be taken to separate the Boiler Works from the Engineering Works. At that time the 300 strong Boiler Works workforce was fully (and profitably) engaged in a variety of fabrication work and it was therefore felt that the time was right to (as it was put) 'slacken' the knot and allow the Boiler Works (now re-named the Fabrication Works) to develop separately. The responsibility for carrying this initiative forward rested with Boiler Works Manager, Joe Craig. He outlined proposals to expand the facility to engage in a more diverse range of fabrications seeking work from other companies so that the facility would be less tied to JBE. That same year the Plating Shop was likewise re-constituted as a separate profit centre under its Manager, George Dalgleish.

---

i   *The Times* (1966), 26 July, p17.
ii   Shipbuilding Industry Committee (1966), *Shipbuilding Industry Committee 1965-66: Report*, March.
iii *JB Newsletter* (1966), No.1, October.
iv   Although JBE had started manufacturing components for their first two gas turbines, this diversification was still in its infancy. On taking up his new post, Bill requested that his job title be Technical Manager and not Gas Turbine Manager, to allow him the flexibility to become involved in other areas of activity if this proved necessary.

3   Marine Engines and Gas Turbines: JBE seeks its markets

Marine Engine Work

Once JBE's structure and personnel were in place, the immediate priority was to find new work to supplement the rapidly dwindling workload inherited from the Shipyard. In the first *Newsletter*, Graham Strachan stated that JBE would seek orders for steam, gas and water turbines, for gearing, diesel engines, marine boilers, heavy fabrication, pressure vessels and any other general engineering work. Crucially, he commented that although in the year prior to separation at least 60 per cent of the manufactured goods coming from the Engine Works had been for customers other than the Shipyard, he warned that they could not now expect preferential treatment from the Shipyard: all work must now be competitive or the Shipyard would take its work elsewhere. The reverse, as he pointed out, was also true in that JBE did not now require to trade with the shipyard and would look for work from, for example, ship owners, public utility companies, oil and chemical companies and general engineering businesses.

Firstly, however, it was necessary to complete the existing marine work: basically somewhat of a 'mixed bag' of water turbines, one Doxford diesel engine, some Sulzer diesel engines and a small amount of general engineering work. Apart from the water turbines and diesel marine engines, their other main work at the time was the manufacture of steam turbines for installation in the *QE2*: the separation agreement had included (as well as contractual responsibility) the transfer to JBE of all outstanding marine engineering work, including the completion of the *QE2* turbines. In addition, they also had a limited amount of admiralty work including the manufacture of specialised CODAG and COGAS gearboxes for installation in Navy frigates. As far as marine and general engineering work was concerned the responsibility for completing the existing work, and for finding new work, fell to the Sales Manager, James Turner. His section duly completed all outstanding orders including the ill-fated *QE2* turbines but thereafter struggled to win new orders for the standard steam and diesel engine types that had been the basic source of income for many years.

Graham Strachan, Managing Director JBE 1969-83

In fact, JBE withdrew from diesel engine manufacture as early as 1967. This was partly because there was at that time a glut in the market, caused by too many diesel engine manufacturers chasing too few orders. Also, the layout of the Works was insufficient to allow the manufacture of diesel engines, in addition to gas and steam turbines. The decision was therefore taken to concentrate solely on steam and gas turbine work, as it was felt that these involved broadly similar operations, necessitating the use of rotating machinery. In order to strengthen their steam turbine activities, JBE signed joint Manufacturing Agreements with both Stal Laval of Sweden, and GE. However, shortly afterwards 75 per cent of this market was lost when Stal Laval entered into a similar agreement with a UK competitor. In the event, they only secured a few minor steam turbine contracts from UCS (Clydebank Division).

The QE2 in the fitting out basin, as a gas turbine leaves Clydebank for America, 1967

The company's most prestigious steam turbine contract (and one of their last) was undoubtedly for the Clydebank-built *QE2*. Unfortunately, however, it was bedevilled by design problems, which created a media storm that threatened the very survival of the new company. The major problem concerned the reliability of the two 55,000shp steam turbine engines - at that time, the most powerful in the world. Unfortunately, the turbines had begun to show signs of excessive vibration whilst the ship was undergoing her final acceptance trials, during a fourteen-day cruise to West Africa in December 1968. These problems, noticed on Christmas Eve by the JBE engineers on board, were almost immediately picked up by the world's media, resulting in headlines such as *The Shame of the Clyde* and *Ship of*

Shame Limps Home.[i] The resulting dispute over liability between Cunard (the ship's owners), UCS and JBE ensued for months thereafter. On inspection, it was discovered that some turbine blades had sheared off and others were cracked, all of which required to be replaced at great expense. After a thorough investigation (involving an independent arbiter and marine specialists) lasting approximately three months, it was found that the damage had been caused by a phenomenon known as steam excited vibration, which was only eliminated by modifying the design of the blades. Although ultimately JBE were cleared of any blame, the unfavourable press coverage proved a serious setback to the young company, and caused many sleepless nights at Board level.

This experience, together with the collapse of their diesel engine market in 1967, led JBE in 1970 to almost completely withdraw from the marine engine market. The one exception was a short-lived joint venture between GE and several of its MAs to instal a marine version of the Frame 3 gas turbine in five vessels owned by the Union Steamship Company of New Zealand Limited. The world's first operational vessel so fitted was the 4,500 ton roll on-roll off cargo ship, *Seaway Prince*. Equipped with a JBE-built marine gas turbine, it was initially more cost-effective than the traditional diesel engines but, like the four other vessels fitted with this marine gas turbine, quickly lost this advantage when the price of gas increased. After the complete withdrawal from marine engine work, Jim Turner was put in charge of the newly-established Contract Administration Department within the main company, and his team of workers was dispersed throughout the rest of the Works.

The move into Gas Turbine Manufacture

In the early 1960s, at the same time as they were taking steps to set up JBE, the London Board was also taking a crucial decision on whether to enter into a Manufacturing Associate (MA) Agreement with the American engineering giant GE, to manufacture heavy duty industrial gas turbines under licence.

GE, formed in 1892 out of a merger of Edison, Sprague and Thomson Houston, had been one of the early pioneers in gas turbine technology and by the mid-1960s was the acknowledged world leader in this field. By 1965, its development was such that, with approximately 400,000 employees and an annual turnover of $7bn, it was generating profits of between $200 and $300m per annum. Although 80 per cent of GE's gas turbine orders at this time were for American customers, the growing international market encouraged the GE Gas Turbine Department (GEGTD) to establish a new section, International General Electric Export (IGE), headed by Manager, Bernie Foye. One of Bernie's first tasks was to establish joint MA Agreements, a concept first proposed by colleague Whit Ridgway.

Around this time, another John Brown subsidiary, CJB, was working in Algeria on several major pipeline contracts which required gas turbine compressor stations to drive the gas through the pipelines. IGE had been attempting to gain a share of this market by supplying the gas turbines for these projects. This was unsuccessful, mainly because British national credits were partly funding the projects (giving British companies an edge in tendering). Consequently, (and on the advice of CJB officials), Bernie Foye contacted John Brown & Company (Clydebank) Limited and their personnel met senior management in Clydebank in November 1964, to discuss establishing a UK MA Agreement. A reciprocal visit was made to GE at Schenectady. Within John Brown there were reservations at both Board and local

Relaxing after early discussions between (left to right) Graham Strachan, IGE Manager Bernie Foye, and Bill Connell

levels, resulting from the financial problems that arose from the Company's earlier venture into the gas turbine field. However, it was clear that since then the reliability of the newer gas turbine models had vastly improved, and this, together with the growing demand for gas turbines, encouraged the Group to re-consider. The eventual decision to proceed with the MA Agreement was undoubtedly one of the most significant ever taken by John Brown & Company Limited. It was signed on 27 May 1965 by John Brown's Engineering Director, Graham Strachan, and GE's Export Sales Manager, Bob Naples. Initially, the Agreement covered a period of seven years (it was renewed in 1972 for a further ten years) and covered only Frame 3 and Frame 5 gas turbines. The story goes that during the negotiations, and before the Agreement was signed, an enquiry was made as to John Brown's financial position. In answer, George Strachan presented the delegation with five single £1 Clydesdale Bank notes showing a ship entering a newly-opened Clydebank Dock, declaring in jest that the company was "one of the few firms that printed its own £1 bank notes"![ii]

Other MAs (popularly referred to as GE's 'string of pearls') in addition to JBE, included Nuovo Pignone (Italy), Thomasson (Holland), Societe Alsthom (France), AEG Fabriken Essen (Germany), Kvaerner Brug (Norway) and Hitachi (Japan). The essence of the MA Agreement was that the MA gained access to the best technology in the world, thus enabling it to compete with rivals in the gas turbine market, such as Brown Boveri, Westinghouse, Pratt & Whitney and Rolls Royce. By some very astute marketing, GE not only set up manufacturers of its own technology to compete against other technologies, but also to compete amongst themselves. Uniquely, purchasers were thus able to specify GE technology knowing that competitive tendering was assured. In this way GE, who supplied the main components of the gas turbines to its MAs, was able to maximise the sale of its own products.

As an MA, John Brown & Company (Clydebank) Limited (and later JBE) was able to build gas turbines, with GE providing a guarantee of performance. It proved far more successful than the licences entered into by American rivals, Westinghouse, with companies such as Fiat. Additionally, the MA concept found ready acceptance from international customers who wanted GE technology, but who could not access it because of national credit and other restrictions. For JBE, the MA Agreement was the key to everything it did in the gas turbine field.

Having signed the Agreement, the first priority was to address various deficiencies, principally in the layout of the Engine Works, and in terms of working attitudes. While the workers possessed the necessary skills, there was concern that the productivity at Clydebank was relatively low in comparison with GE workers. It was also felt that workers lacked the necessary discipline to enable them to meet shipping deadlines. More worryingly, although the Engine Works layout could be re-organised to accommodate an assembly line operation, the company lacked the necessary staff to programme production in a cost effective manner, and apply quality control and testing procedures throughout the sub-assembly and final assembly operations.

Following JBE's withdrawal from the marine engineering market, the future of JBE fell onto the shoulders of Bill Connell and his staff in the Industrial Gas Turbine (IGT) Division. Fortunately, they had little trouble in securing their

Engine Works Bay 1, where the final assembly of the gas turbines took place

first gas turbines orders: their new trading partner GE quickly consolidated the MA Agreement by placing an order for two heavy duty industrial gas turbines worth £600,000 for American utility companies based in Oakwood, Illinois, and Kirksville, Missouri. These initial orders, and a further seven or eight also placed by GE, marked the first phase of JBE's foray into gas turbine production. These were effectively re-imports, that is orders where the principal components of the gas turbine were manufactured in America and shipped across to Clydebank to be fitted into Clydebank-built gas turbines, which were then re-imported into America to be supplied to GE customers. In part, these orders were placed because GE was unable at that time to satisfy the sudden surge in demand for gas turbines from American utility companies, which had been badly shaken by a series of power shortages or 'brown outs'. The most infamous of these 'brown outs' was when New York's *Big Allis*, a huge steam turbine generator, failed on 9 November 1965, causing widespread chaos over the entire state. The strength of the gas turbine was that, in the event of a system failure such as that which occurred with *Big Allis*, a gas turbine (unlike steam) could have the system up and running again in ten minutes. While these 'brown outs' lasted, gas turbines sold like hot cakes, especially during the peak buying month of August. Although this boom was short lived, it nevertheless gave JBE a chance to enter the gas turbine market at an earlier opportunity than might normally have been possible. Furthermore, with GE busy satisfying its own domestic market, it allowed JBE and the other MAs an opportunity to expand their sales activities in the international market.

Gas Turbine 103 for Missouri Power & Light, leaving Clydebank in late 1967

Gas turbine 103 negotiating the railway bridge at Anniesland, Glasgow

Of the first five Frame 5 gas turbines ordered between 1967-68, four were for the American utility companies Connecticut Light & Power Company, Illinois Power Company, Missouri Power & Light Company and Commonwealth Edison. The fifth was for a GE customer in Guatemala. With the exception of the first two, these were built as Advance Orders to reduce delivery time, in the hope that further orders from GE would follow! The initial two gas turbines had been manufactured without confirmation orders having been received. However, while it was exhilarating for the company to be building gas turbines worth several hundred thousand pounds each, there was considerable nervousness about the absence of written confirmation. Accordingly, Alaister Forsyth was sent to Schenectady to obtain the necessary signatures and constant faxes were sent to him from Clydebank seeking daily progress reports. Any nervousness was replaced with pride on Wednesday, 7 June 1967, when the first Clydebank-built gas turbine left JBE en route to the Illinois Power Company's Vermillion plant. An eighty-ton unit worth quarter of a million pounds, it was transported by low load trailer to Finnieston Dock in Glasgow by way of Anniesland Cross, thus avoiding the Whiteinch Tunnel interchange which had insufficient headroom.[iii] The precise route these shipments followed was, of necessity, subject to strict Police control, but generally was by way of Glasgow Road, Alderman Road, Anniesland Road and then along Great Western Road, before proceeding down Byres Road. At the Dock the turbine was loaded onto the freighter *Ardnia*.

Gas Turbine 103 at King George V Dock, Glasgow

The concept of advance ordering followed by GE and others in the gas turbine industry, although risky, played a crucial role in Clydebank's development, and continued throughout the lifetime of JBE, at least for the smaller gas turbine models. Since on average a gas turbine could take eighteen months to manufacture, commencing manufacture in advance of order frequently allowed JBE to supply customers with gas turbines in as little as twelve weeks. For customers urgently requiring gas turbines, or associated equipment such as generators (also manufactured in advance of order), this was a strong selling point and often secured orders for JBE at the expense of its competitors. It was also the main reason why power producers turned to gas turbines for production rather than the more conventional thermal generation systems utilising steam. Whilst advance ordering was extremely useful when the market was buoyant, the risks became clear in the frequent down turns in the gas turbine market. On such occasions, having invested considerable amounts of time and money, JBE faced the prospect of scrapping or dismantling unsold turbines (to sell for parts), or trying to interest potential customers in what was effectively an outdated model. Despite this, it was felt that the advantages outweighed the disadvantages, although the practice created cash flow problems for the company on many occasions.

As well as adapting to GE's production practices, JBE also had to manufacture gas turbines to the required standard. To this end, GE initially monitored JBE's performance, and sent a resident co-ordinator (Roy Heath) to Clydebank to do this, and to ensure standards were met. Roy's job was essentially to inspect all the drawings and process specifications, to ensure that the manufacture of the gas turbine was compatible with GE standards, and that the completed gas turbine met all the relevant factory tests.

There were also other contacts between the new partners, and individuals such as Whit Ridgway and Bob Naples became well known faces at JBE. On Wednesday, 29 November 1967, for example two GE personnel, G.A. File and A.A. Miller, visited Clydebank to discuss, amongst other matters, the Advance Order Stock Programme, the bulk shipment of hardware, cycle times and the required delivery dates for accessory items and substitution procedures. The latter was a contentious item, as GE insisted that all materials used which were different from their specification, be approved by them first. JBE, on the other hand, felt that for certain very minor changes, this was bureaucratic and unnecessary. Ultimately, GE conceded that the mandatory items list for accessories was no longer binding and that JBE should seek UK suppliers where possible.

(Left to right) Bob Naples (GE Manager International Sales), Jack Gatzemeyer (General Manager, GE's Gas Turbine Division), and JBE's Graham Strachan and Bill Connell

As the end of the decade neared, JBE received the 'Oscar' of the GE power world! In 1968, JBE had sold twenty gas turbines. Accordingly, they were judged to be the top performer of all of GE's six MAs, and in February 1969 Graham Strachan received the bronze plaque from GE's Marketing Manager, Howard M. Perry. In 1970, JBE won the GE Award for Manufacturing Associate of the Year, for the second year in a row. This time the award recognised the securing by JBE of £11m worth of gas turbine orders in the preceding year.

Notwithstanding their early successes, the management of the embryonic IGT Department in the first few years had been rather haphazard. There was, for example, no formal divisional structure in the first two years. In these early years, Bill Connell, Alaister Forsyth and Derek Bateman (a draughtsman and engineer) shared a small office. Surprisingly, there was no electrical engineer - until Dan Thompson joined the firm to assist Alaister in setting up an Electrical and Mechanical Group around 1969. Other developments also initiated at this time included the establishment of a Test Group, a Spare Parts Department, a Service Department and an installation service. The first formal Sales appointment was in 1970, when Gordon Wall was recruited from Hawker Siddeley to fill the newly-created post of Sales Manager of the IGT Department.

---

i   Strachan, Graham (n.d.), unpublished and unfinished memoirs.
ii   Strachan, Graham (n.d.), unpublished and unfinished memoirs.
iii   *Clydebank Press* (1967), 9 June, p11.

4 The Development of Gas Turbine Work

Manufacturing for Clients other than GE

Despite initially benefiting from GE re-imports, Graham Strachan and Bill Connell were well aware that they could not rely entirely on GE for work. Throughout 1967 they directed a concerted sales effort to secure gas turbine orders from other potential customers in Commonwealth countries such as Canada, Australia and New Zealand. A series of sales presentations was accordingly undertaken in, for example, Wellington, New Zealand, and Brisbane, Sydney, Melbourne, Adelaide and Perth in Australia. The following year, similar visits were made to the Middle East (partly to promote the concept of waste heat for desalination applications) and the Caribbean, with further visits being planned for Switzerland and East and West Pakistan.

The company won fifteen contracts in the late 1960s, bringing the total gas turbines ordered to date to forty-two. While slightly less than half were GE re-imports (again mostly for American utility companies), significantly the remaining contracts included orders from Brunei, Puerto Rico, the Bahamas, and the Middle East. The first Middle Eastern power generation order was secured in January 1968 and was an extremely important breakthrough, as over the years this market proved to be the most productive for the company. The contract, for the Ministry of Water & Electricity Department of the United Arab Emirates, was initially for two Frame 5 gas turbines, generators, control panels, and various other accessories. These were for a power plant in Abu Dhabi, engineered by consultants, Ewbank & Partners. A further three Frame 5 turbines were also ordered that year. The first two turbines were shipped out to Abu Dhabi the following year. While the power station was being built, the first turbine was modified to allow for operation on a temporary outdoor site to meet the urgent need for power.

The Aluminium Bahrain Smelter complex *JBE gas turbines at the Smelter complex*

In late 1968 a massive order was received from Aluminium Bahrain (ALBA) for nine Frame 5 gas turbines for their new Aluminium Smelter Plant. ALBA had been established solely to operate the smelter, and had as its major shareholder the Bahrain government. Seemingly, the idea for this smelter arose from a casual remark made at a New York luncheon party in 1968 by a surveyor looking at opportunities for 'new-type' industries in Bahrain, to a banker sitting beside him who was assisting a group of aluminium users and brokers then looking for a site for an aluminium smelter. As was said at that time "somewhere between the soup and the soufflé"[i] came the idea of an aluminium smelter in Bahrain.

Traditionally, because the extraction of aluminium required vast uninterrupted amounts of electricity, such smelters were normally built where there was access to cheap and reliable hydro-electric power. However, the availability of abundant natural gas reserves in Bahrain made the use of gas turbines highly economical. At that time, Bahrain was preparing for independence from Britain the following year, and the British government was offering some commercial support to Bahrain to compensate for its withdrawal. Accordingly, entrepreneurs like Paul Brauner (the Chief Executive of Amari Limited, a buyer of prime aluminium ingots, who would later work with JBE in Dubai Aluminium) and Nick Cutteridge (a merchant banker) reasoned that funds might be made available to Bahrain to allow the construction of the smelter. The smelter would process alum into aluminium. Since this accounted for only about 20 per cent of the cost of aluminium production, this, together with the fairly negligible cost of utilising the local natural gas, would give the smelter a major competitive advantage. Accordingly, a British consortium (British Smelter Construction Limited) comprising Amari Limited, George Wimpey & Company Limited and JBE, was formed to secure the contract for all constructional work and the supply of the gas turbines and associated equipment. The contract was signed in 1968, with Wimpey carrying out all civil engineering works, JBE supplying the gas turbines, and Amari providing the smelting plant and technical expertise. Once operational, the turbines gobbled up 100 million cubic feet of gas per day.

Gudvin Tofte, General Manager of ALBA, is presented with a silver tray by JBE Operations Director, Alaister Forsyth (on the right), to mark the completion of the one million fired hours of operation, 1979

In 1969, a further order followed for another five units (making a total of fourteen in all). On 11 September 1969 the Chairman of ALBA, John Dennis Robbins, visited Clydebank to personally inspect the first of the fourteen units and, hinted that further expansion might create further opportunities for additional turbines. True to his word, an order for a further four was placed in 1970. When the £62m aluminium smelter was officially opened in May 1971 by his Highness Sheikh Isa bin Sulman Al-Khalifa pouring the first ingot of aluminium, it was capable of producing 120,000 tons of aluminium each year. This was a highly significant order for JBE on three counts. Firstly, the eighteen gas turbines represented by far the largest single order the company had ever undertaken at that time. Secondly, it was then the largest gas turbine power station in the world, and thirdly, it was the first time that gas turbines had been used for the smelting of aluminium.

The presentation of JBE's first Queens Award to Chairman Sir George Gardner (on the right) by Lord Lieutenant Robert Arbuthnott, 1970. Graham Strachan stands on the left.

JBE Secretarial staff at the Queens Award presentation ceremony, 1970

In early March 1969, a £6m batch of orders from the USA and Canada had been announced. Including the ALBA turbines, this meant an order book of £20m won since 1966, and guaranteed full employment for the IGT Division until into the mid-1970s. In addition, in September 1969 the company had secured a further £2.5m of orders for seven units. Six of these units were for Puerto Rico (this was said to be JBE's first Latin American order); the other – a single Frame 5 – was destined for the millionaire's playground, Nassau (this latter order having been placed by the Bahamas Electricity Corporation).

A further turbine order came out of the ALBA project in 1972, making a final total of nineteen gas turbines for that particular project: quite rightly regarded by Alaister Forsyth (who project managed the contract for a few years) as a fabulous achievement by the fledgling company.

On 10 June 1970, in the presence of Provost James Queenan of Clydebank and other invited guests, Sir George Gardner, Chairman of JBE, addressed the workforce on the occasion of their winning their first Queens Award to Industry for securing £25m of orders for gas turbines in the preceding three years. In accepting the Award from the Lord Lieutenant, Robert Arbuthnott, Sir George announced that a further £5m of orders had been won for twelve gas turbines, eleven of which were destined for American customers. Clearly

JBE Far East Sales Manager, Nigel Hill, with Vice-Premier Wang Zhen at the 1979 China Energy Show in Beijing

moved by JBE's performance, Sir George described the moment as "a golden wreath to add to the crown of a Royal hour".[ii] Robert Arbuthnott, a former locomotive engineer, for his part confessed to a feeling of nostalgia occasioned by the smell of the works and declared that "no ceremony had given him greater pleasure".[iii] Fittingly this was one of the last duties for Sir George, for a few month's later he announced his retirement. Sir George, who had been Chairman of JBE since its inception in October 1966, was succeeded by his Deputy, John A.R. Staniforth, CBE. John Staniforth (commonly known as 'JAR'), who took up office on 14 October, was then a Director of John Brown & Company Limited, Managing Director of Constructors John Brown, and had been a Director of JBE since 1968.

Around May 1970 JBE won a contract to supply one Frame 5 gas turbine to the China Light & Power Company Limited to upgrade their Hok Un Power Station in Kowloon, Hong Kong. The principal player in this had been JBE's Regional Sales Manager for the Far East and Australia, Nigel Hill. Having been brought up in Surabaja in the Dutch East Indies, where his father had a plantation, he was fluent in Malay, Javanese, Dutch and Mandarin. After helping to run the family business, Nigel had undertaken various consultancy positions before finally joining JBE in 1968 as a Senior Project Engineer. In 1970 he was appointed Regional Sales Manager - Far East, and was active in promoting the sale of gas turbines in Burma, Borneo and China. Reputedly, while patiently negotiating over many months with representatives of China Light in order to secure this contract, Nigel was almost posted 'missing in action' by his concerned colleagues in Clydebank. Much to their relief, he re-appeared with an order worth just under £1m - and the promise of further ones! The order had been won following a visit to the Hok Un Power Station by Nigel. Having enquired about a derelict building alongside their 90mw steam plant, he was told that it contained a 12.5mw steam set which was lying inactive because its boiler was 'finished'. Nigel suggested that perhaps JBE could supply China Light with a gas turbine and new boiler to utilise the waste heat from the gas turbine to produce steam, as well as further enhancements which could improve output. Accordingly, JBE won this contract, in the process seeing off fierce competition from firms such as Hitachi, Westinghouse, Mitsubishi and Brown Boveri. It was the first time JBE had sold a gas turbine generator together with a boiler, to utilise the waste heat from the turbine to provide steam for an existing steam turbine generating set. The gas turbine was shipped out in October 1971, commissioned in February 1972, and the 're-powered' Hok Un Station was officially opened on 29 June 1972.

The winning of this contract was timely for JBE because, despite a prediction by Strachan that the early 1970s would see a steady increase in turnover and employment, in actual fact the only other orders on the books were for seven Frame 5 turbines for Argentina, Algeria and Burma. This represented a substantial reduction from previous years and led to production being scaled down and, in 1972, the imposition of voluntary redundancies. Fortunately, the order proved to be a turning point, for shortly afterwards further orders worth over £20m restored the order book to something like past levels. These orders included the first of the larger Frame 7 combined cycle units, on this occasion ordered by GE for the Korea Electric Company.

In September 1971 the Clydebank Works was one of the venues for a visiting Chinese trade mission organised by the Sino-British Council. The party included Messrs. Chang Tsien-hua (Commercial Counsellor), Yen Ju-tai (Commercial Secretary), Chang Yao-huan, Ying Hui-pi and Wang Hsueh-hsien (all attachés). Also present were P. Marshall, Chinese Secretary of the Sino-British Council, and Allan Dew, Assistant Secretary of the Confederation of British Industry (Scottish Branch). The company had high hopes from the "five neatly blue-clad men, each sporting a distinctive star-shaped red badge, who toured the GT production bays".[iv] Clearly interested in buying British goods, the Chinese delegation took away an abundance of literature, leaving the distinct impression that, given the right deal, JBE could secure work in what had, up till then, been something of a closed market to western companies.

The breaching of the 'bamboo curtain' came on 19 December 1971 and marked yet another major milestone in the history of JBE. On that day Bill Connell and Nigel Hill signed a £3.5m contract (the company's first in the People's Republic of China) for the supply of five Frame 5 power plants. Bill Connell was fascinated by China, and had quickly sensed the huge potential of this market. China at that time was largely a closed market and difficult to get into and, as a consequence, many people doubted that Bill would be able to make inroads into China. That JBE did was a source of great satisfaction to him: apparently, after the signing of this contract, Bill came back home from China around 2 o'clock in the morning with a Chinese hat on his head and waving a contract saying, "I've done it. I've done it".[v]

Immediately the contract was signed, a 'China' team headed by Nigel Hill began (both in Clydebank and Beijing) to firm up proposals for the supply of the power plants. At the same time, production began at Clydebank. In 1972, during the course of construction, engineers from Machimpex visited Clydebank to inspect progress on the turbines. A civic reception (hosted by Clydebank's Provost, Robert Fleming) to acknowledge the cordial relations between JBE and China was given on Friday, 17 March. At this the tables were decorated with yellow chrysanthemums in honour of the visiting party. Also present was John Staniforth and other invited guests. Being Saint Patrick's Day, the Chinese delegation had each been presented on arrival with a sprig of shamrock by Aer Lingus stewardesses.

Although the turbines were completed ahead of schedule, their shipment was delayed for two months by a dockers' strike that paralysed British ports throughout June and July. The

A consignment of elbowed inlet ducts for China negotiating the railway bridge at Anniesland, Glasgow

Top: Gas turbines and elbowed inlet ducts at Stobcross Quay prior to shipping out, 1972
Bottom: Loading of gas turbine on the Danish freighter, Titan Scan, 1972

86 ton turbines, and components, finally left the Clydebank Works in late 1972 - on an articulated low loader with a police escort. The first one to be transported was not, however, without mishap for en-route to Stobhill Quay the police escort was obliged to chase after a reported stolen car, leaving the low loader stranded at the roadside! There were also difficulties with the seventeen-and-a-half foot high elbowed inlet ducts being transported, as most of the bridges on the possible routes to the quay side had insufficient height to allow passage. Finally, however, all of the equipment was hoisted aboard a Danish freighter for shipment to London, before being transferred onto another ship for passage to China. Nigel

Hill, who accompanied the consignment in order to supervise the unloading of the equipment in China, was later forced to try and explain the delay to the Chinese clients although, as he remarked: "The Chinese have no experience of strikes. If a worker did go on strike he would probably starve, since in China everyone is issued with a card with which to buy provisions. If a worker showed a 'strike card' he would be turned away from shops empty handed".[vi]

Packaged Power Plants: JBE takes another step forward

By 1968 the outlook for potential gas turbine work had been sufficiently clear to allow the company to re-structure. In that year the company had formed two main Divisions, namely the IGT Division and a Marine & General Engineering (later Marine & Compressor) Division.

This re-structuring preceded a further phase in the company's development. Up until then, Clydebank had concentrated solely (and, some felt, correctly) on the manufacture of 'stand alone' gas turbines. However, increasingly the market was demanding what was termed 'packaged' units, comprising a gas turbine and a generator or compressor. Bill Connell and his men determined to meet this new demand. Accordingly, in 1967 various suppliers were sounded out regarding the supply of generators and compressors.

The preferred supplier for generators was Brush Electrical Machines Limited of Leicester. Part of the Hawker Siddeley Group, Brush guaranteed to manufacture generators in advance of order. They could therefore deliver generators to JBE within periods of as little as eighteen weeks, instead of the usual two years, thus matching JBE's advance order programme. This was a brave move on the part of Brush, since the cost of generators for Frame 5 applications would then average around £100,000. However, it spawned a long and fruitful association for both companies that lasted from 1968, when Brush supplied two 2 pole generators for the Bangkapi Power Station in Thailand, until 1993. During that period, Brush supplied JBE with almost three hundred generators, by far the majority being supplied between 1968 and 1986, after which generator orders became more sporadic. This lengthy relationship developed into more than simply a business relationship, and Managing Director, John Durber (affectionately known as 'Mac'), was a frequent, and welcome, visitor to Clydebank and a participant in the numerous company golf outings.

Anthony Grant MP with NUGMW Shop Stewards Convener Richard Maxwell, and colleague, 1970

The intention of JBE to manufacture its own compressors was announced on 8 December 1970 by Trade and Industry Minister, Anthony Grant MP, during a visit to Clydebank, and

The signing of the letter of intent for JBE's first packaged power plant, Thailand, 1968.
Present are (left to right) Nai Kasame Chatikavanij, General Manager of the Yanhee Electricity Authority; JBE Managing Director, Graham Strachan; and Nai Patiphat Arayasastra, Deputy General Manager, Yanhee.

The two packaged power plants at the Bangkok North site, Thailand

manufacture of a range of Dresser-Clark compressors began the following year, when JBE entered into a joint venture agreement with Dresser. A separate Compressor Department within the now re-named Marine & Compressor Division[vii] was established: the new Department occupied an area known as the 'quarter-deck', which had once been used as Estimating Offices by the Shipyard. It was headed by Ian Broadley and included, in addition to JBE staff, two Dresser-Clark personnel: Carl Finley and Derek Badland (to be followed by Stewart Nisbet). By Spring 1971, the first of five compressors which had been ordered was operating on a site in Ambergate in Derbyshire to boost the flow of natural gas from the North Sea fields to the UK National Grid. At that time the Department had an order book of £500,000 for compressors for English, North African and Middle East markets, including several centrifugal gas booster compressors ordered by Dresser for the Gas Council in Britain, and Brefcon/Petrobras of Brazil. Three other compressors were ordered by Fluor/Sonatrach of Algeria for use with process machinery in an Algerian petro-chemical plant. The largest order at that time was for five two-stage boosters for the National Iranian Oil Corporation (IMEG) for a natural gas pipeline project. In addition, JBE supplied type 463B4-4 centrifugal gas compressors for installations in the North Sea's Viking and Thistle Fields. In 1972, JBE prepared to test the latest Dresser compressor unit, ultimately destined for Newfoundland. This ability to now supply both gas turbine generator and compressor sets was a sign of JBE's growing maturity in the international gas turbine market.

In November 1967, Bill Connell and his team secured an order from the Yanhee Electricity Authority for two packaged power plants for sites near Bangkok. This contract was doubly significant: it was won, not through GE, but in open competition and also it involved (in addition to the supply of two Frame 5 gas turbine units) the supply, shipping and installation of a filter house, ducting, control cab, generator, some switch gear and a transformer. In effect JBE was being asked for the first time in its short history to undertake the role of a 'turnkey contractor', that is, to design and build complete (albeit small) power plants. It was a huge breakthrough, demonstrating to GE and competitors, that JBE had the ability to operate at the highest level. GE were delighted with the deal, as they had always envisaged JBE (like other MAs) could be more than a GE sub-contractor, and could play a fuller role, enhancing GE's reputation in the process. In 1968 all the equipment was shipped out from Glasgow, and shortly afterwards the contract was successfully completed within the agreed timescale. The location of one of the sites, Bangkapi, presented particular problems: the gas turbine was to rest on top of concrete piles that had to be driven (with great difficulty) into a paddy field. Further, as there was no access road to the site, a temporary road had to be laid by the JBE site engineers, and the turbine 'skidded' into position along metal covered timbers. However, once installed, the turbine reputedly operated so quietly that families living within fifty yards of the plant said that they could sleep undisturbed at night! The overall success of the contract meant that a repeat order was secured for a further two Frame 5 units in 1968, for the Bangkok South site.

Up until 1971 JBE's penetration into the Far East and Australasian market had been confined to Brunei, Hong Kong, Thailand and Australia, but further inroads were made in September 1971 when, in the face of fierce competition, JBE picked up their first Burmese order. This order (worth £3.2m) was for the supply of a 60mw gas turbine power station for Chauk for the Electricity State Board of Burma. In addition to supplying three heavy-duty industrial gas turbines with Brush generators, JBE were to undertake all necessary survey

JBE-built gas turbines on board Z103 en route to Chauk, Burma

work, and construct a turbine hall, switch gear annexe and control room. This turnkey contract was signed in Rangoon by Financial Director, Peter B. Low, and Contracts Manager, Jack Bell. As well as being JBE's first contract in Burma, two other aspects ensured that it would be forever memorable. Firstly, the method of payment! The Burmese government did not have sufficient hard cash to pay for this project and therefore the competing bidders tried to entice the Burmese government with various low interest credits or other deals. JBE took a different tack. Acting through a company associated with Lewis & Peat's Commodity and General Merchanting Group, an approach was made to the UK's Foreign and Commonwealth Office to persuade it to purchase £2m worth of rice from the Burmese government (they, in turn, would use this rice as part of a £6m UK aid package to Pakistan). This ingenious proposal was accepted and the contract was awarded to JBE. The other unusual feature concerned the difficulties in transporting the turbines and all other necessary equipment 400 miles up the Irrawaddy River to its destination at Chauk. In the event, in 1972 the three turbines - each weighing eighty tons - were loaded onto a 'Z' craft and transported up the river during the monsoon season, when water levels were high. One official who experienced the problems at first hand was Charlie Kirkpatrick, JBE's Burmese Project Co-ordination Manager for three years. Based at Rangoon, Charlie and his men had to battle constantly against the effects of the monsoon climate, which for five months in every year left sites like quagmires, making it almost impossible to use the heavy site equipment. Their greatest problem was the Irrawaddy itself, since the river level in the monsoon period often rose by more than 60 feet, causing it to overflow its banks. While offloading equipment at this time was comparatively easy, it was a different story when the levels dropped. Then the problem of unloading heavy equipment from the 'Z' craft up steep river banks produced many 'nail biting' moments. Despite these problems, the project was successfully completed at the beginning of 1974.

The Burma contract was not the only time in the company's history that rice has featured! It was standard practice, when the performance of a gas turbine in the test bay or on site was less than satisfactory, and contamination or fouling of the compressor blades was suspected, for a few pounds of American long grain rice to be fed into the gas turbine air inlet to remove the contamination. Indeed, this practice was recommended by GE. Thus JBE used a particular Glasgow shop where quantities of this rice could be purchased. When Chinese and other Asian visitors were visiting the firm, and staying in self-catering accommodation, JBE personnel often gave their guests bags of rice for their evening meals!

In the spring of 1972 the company were able to announce they had won a "double yoked Golden Easter Egg":[viii] two orders worth a total of £2.4m. The first, for the supply of a 24mw gas turbine and associated equipment and worth £1m, was announced during the visit to Clydebank by His Excellency Shebib Al Zahiri, under-secretary to the Minister of Water and Electricity in Abu Dhabi. Graham Strachan commented that it was most appropriate that the company's 100th gas turbine was for Abu Dhabi since this had also been the destination for JBE's first two base load gas turbines back in 1968. The second order was for two 16mw gas turbine packaged power plants for Crete. The negotiations for this order (the first awarded to a UK company by Greece's Public Power Corporation for many years) were conducted by JBE Commercial Manager, Donald MacLeod, and Regional Sales Manager, Robert Steel. The following month Bill Connell flew to Athens and, in the company of Mr. Demopoulus (Governor of the Public Power Corporation), the Greek Deputy Premier, Mr. Macarezos, and Sir Robin Hooper, the British Ambassador, signed the agreement to enable the £1.4m contract to proceed.

JBE: the progress so far ...
At its beginning, the company had been little more than a sub-contractor for GE, solely engaged in the manufacture of small heavy duty industrial gas turbines. Quickly, it had progressed, firstly to supplying packaged power units which comprised (in addition to gas turbines) generators, compressors and associated equipment, and, secondly, to

undertaking the role of turnkey contractor responsible for (in addition to supplying gas turbines and other equipment) the design, construction and installation of complete power plants. By the end of its first ten years in operation, JBE were producing a range of gas turbines of 6 - 100mw capacity for power generation, and had become one of the largest gas turbine manufacturers outside of the US.

Analysis of gas turbine sales up to and including 1976 showed a fairly even geographical spread, with fifty units sold in Europe (including Russia), thirty-two in Africa, sixty-three in the Middle East, thirty-one in the Far East, and fifty-five in North and South America. Perhaps surprisingly, less than twenty turbines were supplied to the UK and North Sea markets. Out of this total of 250 units, 136 were for power generation, 92 for mechanical drive applications and 22 for offshore platform and marine drive operations. Overall there had been an increase in production, with the annual numbers of gas turbines manufactured at Clydebank showing a steady growth from nil in March 1967, to five in 1968, fifteen in 1970, twenty-three in 1973, and thirty-one in 1976.

By late 1972, the continuing strength of the IGT Division and the growing North Sea offshore market had prompted a major re-structuring of the company that impacted on all aspects of administration, manufacturing, sales and training. The two existing Divisions - Industrial Gas Turbine and Marine & Compressor - were replaced by six new Divisions. Two of these (Engineering and Marketing) were headed by Bill Connell, who became Director and General Manager of both. Jim Turner (having relinquished control of the now defunct Marine & Compressor Division) was made Director of Contract Administration Division; Company Secretary, Allan Gormly, was elected onto the Board of Directors, in addition to heading the Commercial Division; and William Davie and Peter Low were made Directors of the Manufacturing and Financial Divisions respectively. The staff displaced from the IGT and Marine & Compressor Divisions were absorbed throughout the new Divisions.

In essence, this restructuring was designed to meet changing conditions. Since being set up in 1968, the expanding gas turbine business had progressed unhindered by the declining marine business. By 1970, 90 per cent of the company's turnover was in the manufacture of gas turbines and associated equipment.

---

i   *JB Newsletter* (1971), Summer.
ii *JB Newsletter* (1970), Autumn.
iii *JB Newsletter* (1970), Autumn.
iv *JB Newsletter* (1970), Winter.
v   Interview with Mrs. Joan Connell, 15 November 2001.
vi *JB Newsletter* (1972), Autumn.
vii The Marine & Compressor Division was previously known as the Marine & General Engineering Division.
viii *JB Newsletter* (1972), Spring.

5   Oil: A Window of Opportunity

Oil Pipeline Turbines

Because of changing market conditions in the early 1970s (caused by an energy crisis), JBE began to concentrate on the manufacture of Frame 3 and Frame 5 mechanical drive units, instead of the Frame 3 and Frame 5 power generation units, which had been a major part of their business until then. The Frame 3 and Frame 5 mechanical drive units were designed, not to generate electricity, but to drive compressors to pump oil or natural gas through pipelines. JBE had been supplying mechanical drive units since 1967, when they won their first contract - a Frame 5 supplied to the Hague-based Arabian American Oil Company (ARAMCO) for a site in Saudi Arabia. This had been followed almost immediately with the supply of a similar unit (a GE re-import) to Alberta Natural Gas. Thereafter, no Frame 5 mechanical drive units were sold until 1974. In the years between 1968 and 1970, however, six contracts were won to supply Frame 3 mechanical drive units, these being GE re-imports for Esso, Tennessee Gas and the Michigan Wisconsin Pipeline Company. A total of sixteen Frame 3 mechanical drive units were sold between 1968 and 1972.

Graham Strachan (on the left) and Sales Manager, Jim McDowell (with interpreter, Marian Keddalli) during the Algerian pipeline negotiations

Frame 3 JBE-built gas turbines for the Hassi Rimel pipeline project

In 1970 JBE secured a contract from Alsthom on behalf of Sonatrach (the Algerian National Oil Company), and having thus gained a toehold in an Algerian pipeline construction project, JBE were represented for the first time at the 1971 International Trade Fair in Algeria. In January 1973, JBE were awarded a share of a further Algerian pipeline contract secured by sister company, CJB. This contract was for the construction of a 300 mile long 40 inch diameter gas pipeline connecting the gas fields at Hassi Rimel with the coastal town of Skikda (where the gas was liquefied for shipment), and had been won by CJB in late 1972. To ensure a steady flow of gas through the pipeline, two compressor stations were constructed at strategic points along the pipeline each equipped with four Frame 3 mechanical drive gas turbines to drive the compressor units. The contract for the turbines and compressors awarded by CJB to JBE was worth over £4m. In 1974 an order for a further twelve Frame 3 twin shaft mechanical drive gas turbines complete with compressors, for the

*Signing the contract for the Hassi Rimel to Arzew pipeline project.
Present are: (standing) H.J. Hays, Resident Manager Algeria; H.H. Hamra, Senior Vice-President;
H. Brady, Vice-President; M.E. Smith, Purchasing Manager; (sitting) L.A. Burger, Chief Engineer;
Bill Connell; Jim McDowell; and Peter A.W. Winnicott, Regional Sales Manager, JBE.*

Hassi Rimel to Arzew pipeline was placed by the Williams International Group (commonly referred to as Willbros) on behalf of Sonatrach, to increase the capacity of the pipeline from 324bn to 448bn cubic feet per year. JBE's share of this contract represented (at that time) their largest single order for Frame 3 mechanical drive compressor sets and, together with the earlier pipeline orders, took JBE's total share to almost £13m.

In June 1973 JBE received an order, on this occasion worth over £4m, from the Power Gas-Harris Group on behalf of the Abu Dhabi Marine Areas Limited (ADMA) - a

Offshore operations at the Abu Dhabi Marine Areas Limited, Umm Shaif complex

consortium of British Petroleum, Compagnie Francaise Petrole, the Abu Dhabi government and a Japanese consortium of oil companies. The order was for six Frame 5 power generation units for an off-shore installation that would pipe gas from two off-shore platforms to the storage tanks on Das Island - a tiny island measuring three-quarters by half-a-mile. To get on to the island, JBE's staff had to fly in on the quaintly named 'Bechtel bomber'! The consultants, Ewbank and Partners, were responsible for the design and construction of the power plant and two oil platforms.

In late 1974, while in the process of shipping out their 150th gas turbine, IGT won a major order from GE. Placed on behalf of the Russian buying agency, Machinoimport, it was for the supply of twelve of the sixty-five Frame 3 mechanical drive gas turbines required for the Bratsvo pipeline. The full contract required the construction of ten compressor stations equipped with a series of gas turbines designed to pump natural gas through the 48 inch diameter pipeline. Clydebank's share was in itself a significant breakthrough, for this was the first time in its history that JBE had penetrated behind the Iron Curtain to secure gas turbine orders. During construction, the Clydebank Works were visited by two prominent officials from the Soviet Embassy in London: N.V. Ivanov, Head of the USSR Trade Delegation, and V.P. Molotkov, Head of Machinoimport. Although such visits later became commonplace, this was the first time Clydebank had played host to a Russian delegation. As each visit required security clearance from the Government, management had to liaise in advance with Special Branch personnel, and thereafter the movements of the visitors were strictly monitored by Special Branch, and restricted to a fifteen-mile radius of the Clydebank Works.

N.V. Ivanov (centre), Head of USSR Trade Delegation, and V.P. Molotkov (far right), Head of Machinoimport, signing the JBE visitors book. Also present are Graham Strachan (on the left) and John Staniforth (standing)

JBE were able to bask in the winning of a share of a second Russian pipeline order so massive that it literally staggered the gas turbine world: on 12 August 1976,[i] following two years of tough negotiations fighting off strong British and foreign competition, a West German consortium (of which JBEGT was a partner) won an order for 123 Frame 3 compressor sets for a 1,440 mile long pipeline. The pipeline ran from the Orenburg gas field in the former Soviet Union, to Uzhgorod in the Ukraine, near the Czechoslovakian border. It was financed by a $600m Eurodollar loan, the largest ever to the Soviet Union to that date, and was designed to supply Western Europe with cheap natural gas. The pipeline order was placed by Machinoimport. The consortium, which also included AEG-Kanis Turbinenfabrik GMBH and

Mannesman-Export AG (both West Germany), was contracted to construct seventeen compressor stations. The remaining compressor stations were to be built by an Italian consortium (including another GE MA, Nuovo Pignone). Since each of the thirty-three gas turbines placed with JBE was identical, there were no particular manufacturing problems. However, the storage of the completed turbines did require additional space, and this was found within JBLB's old Works at Whitecrook. In 1977 the first twenty-five turbines were shipped out, followed by the remaining eight in April 1978 - one month ahead of schedule. Transportation of these units from Clydebank to Hull was described by Shipping Manager, Douglas McCaw, as a "belt and braces job"[ii]: it involved double teams of drivers, two low loaders (one spare for use in the event of a breakdown), and a back up vehicle crammed with spare parts.

Turbines for the North Sea
From the company's inception, the demand for industrial gas turbines had been increasing annually by approximately 10 to 15 per cent. However, the world energy crisis in 1973 (which had been caused by higher oil costs) resulted in a reduced demand for turbines for power generation. Fortunately, the crisis also encouraged the major oil and gas producers to expand their facilities in order to benefit from the high oil prices. This was particularly so in the North Sea, where there was a substantial increase in investment in oil production equipment. The effect of this change in demand meant that in 1973 orders for gas turbines for power generation decreased to 50 per cent of JBE's total orders, whilst those for North Sea operations increased to 25 per cent.

The growing importance of the North Sea oil industry had first been noted by Graham Strachan in late 1971 in an article in the company's newsletter entitled *Oil - The New Horizon: Can Scotland compete?*.[iii] International environmental concerns were then hindering the extraction of oil in Alaska and the Gulf of Mexico, forcing American oil producers to look elsewhere - one such place being the North Sea. In his view this represented significant opportunities for UK industry in general. However, he felt strongly that Scotland was losing out in this, and was determined to do something about it. At that time, of thirty oil platforms on order (worth a staggering £135m), only one was being built in the UK - in the UCS (Clydebank Division) yard. Other UK yards were, as Graham Strachan put it "hell bent"[iv] on tapping into this market, and he was equally keen that JBE should too. Unfortunately, JBE was unable to construct these particular rigs, which were large self-propelled units more suited to the deep waters off the north east coast of Scotland. However, Graham Strachan believed that they did have the engineering skills and expertise to build either smaller oil rigs or associated fabrications, either on their own, or as part of a consortium. He also saw the opportunity of supplying industrial gas turbines, either for the generation of electricity on the rigs, or for driving compressors to increase the pressure in the oil wells, thereby boosting output. He declared, "For once we have a market on our doorstep".[v]

By early 1972, Graham Strachan's predictions were looking feasible. By then, it was estimated that the major oil producers were looking to spend an average of £50m annually in operating and associated costs over the following ten years. Whilst the Clyde yards could not compete with the deep water oil rig construction yards springing up in the north east of

Scotland, Graham Strachan was prepared to adapt working practices, or take work under licence, in order that JBE secure a share in this oil bonanza. By late 1973, the fruits of JBE's sales endeavours were rewarded when a contract worth £800,000 was secured for two compressor drive units for Phillips Petroleum.

These units, designed to boost the flow of natural gas from BP's East Anglican field to Phillips Petroleum's natural gas terminal at Bacton in Norfolk, were yet another milestone in the company's history, for it was the first time that they had sold a gas turbine for use in Britain. Shortly afterwards further orders worth £4m were received from Mobil (North Sea) Limited for three Frame 5 single shaft gas turbines together with generators for the Beryl field, and from Occidental Petroleum for two units for the Piper field. By 1974, a staggering £23m of contracts had been received by JBE for offshore exploration drilling and production platform work.

A Foray into Fabrication: the story of JBE Offshore Limited

At this time, JBE decided to look into the possibility of setting up a wholly-owned subsidiary (to be called JBE Offshore Limited) solely to construct platform modules, deck sections, pipe bridges, helidecks, crane pedestals, flare booms and boat landings. A factor in the decision to form JBE Offshore Limited had been that sister company CJB were already one of the leaders in the design of offshore jacket legs and top sides, and were then working closely with the oil companies. Whilst CJB continued to design the jacket and top sides, the John Brown Group further profited by allowing JBE Offshore to carry out the aforementioned sub-contracting fabrication work and IGT (later John Brown Engineering Gas Turbines Limited [JBEGT]) to supply the gas turbines. The formation of JBE Offshore therefore would enable the Group uniquely (among UK companies at least) to offer a

JBE Offshore Director, Jim Dickson (fourth from left), with a party including MPs Dr. Jeremy Bray (Motherwell and Wishaw), Dr. Maurice Miller (East Kilbride), James White (Glasgow Pollock) and Ian Campbell (West Dunbartonshire), Spring 1975

complete package for offshore projects. Of the many John Brown subsidiaries, JBE Offshore would carry out this fabrication work for three reasons: (i) it already had a pool of skilled labour undertaking general fabrication; (ii) it shared the site at Clydebank with the Marathon company, which had taken over the former John Brown Shipyard on 8 August 1972 expressly for the manufacture of oil rigs; and (iii) the proximity to docking facilities at Rothesay Dock. In charge of the setting-up of the new company (which included the preparation of a feasibility plan to use Rothesay Dock) was James Dickson. James had been recruited from former associates, Foster Wheeler John Brown, who were then fabricating platform modules in Dumbarton.

By late 1974, with the preliminary work involved in setting-up the company completed, James Dickson, now Director and General Manager, officially announced the creation of six hundred new jobs and an initial order book worth £5m. Despite the promise of much needed jobs, however, not everyone was happy with the proposal to set up a new company in the area. Residents of Whitecrook Street (which was near the company's Whitecrook Works) expressed grave concerns, which were fiercely debated in the local press throughout the first half of 1975. These complaints centred on the use of Whitecrook Street for the movement of the massive oil platform modules from the old JBLB works to Rothesay Dock. Residents were unhappy at the parking restrictions imposed on them, due to the narrowness of the road: instead of using off-street parking, they were obliged to park their vehicles in a supervised area provided by JBE. In addition, there were genuine fears that the weight of the loads would damage underground gas pipes and, in so doing, trigger a gas explosion. Although the local Council (Clydebank District) were generally supportive of JBE Offshore, they did sympathise with the residents, particularly since there had perhaps been a lack of consultation with regard to the parking issue. Pledging to "fight to the death",[vi] an action group was set up by residents to lobby the Scottish Office and local politicians, in order to have the development halted until proper safety checks could be made with regard to the underground gas pipes. In the event, the street was used for many years with no apparent damage being caused.

The JBE Offshore Whitecrook Works   *Inside the West Shed, Whitecrook Works*

Reproduced courtesy of The Herald and Evening Times. Copyright of Newsquest Media Group.

However, the complaints didn't stop there. Once the company was up and running, more followed - this time from residents in Braes Avenue (alongside Whitecrook Works). Around ninety tenants lobbied the Council to complain about the excessive noise created by cranes operating day and night, and to request that the handling of pipes and steel plates be carried out in another part of the stockyard. They also complained about searchlights shining into their houses at all hours, excessive swearing from the workmen, clouds of rust blowing about their gardens and dirtying washing, and difficulties in hearing the sound from their televisions. In addition, they complained of a lack of privacy because the stockyard overlooked their houses giving workers a view into their homes. Although efforts were made by the company to solve the problems raised, ultimately the residents had to put up with a certain amount of inconvenience.

Following JBE Offshore's formation, construction of the module building facility at both Whitecrook and Rothesay Dock had commenced almost immediately. By November 1974 the recruitment of the initial 600 strong workforce had been completed, and a labour agreement (described as "the finest in Europe"[vii]) had been reached between the local Trade Unions and management of JBE Offshore. By June 1975 all the necessary site construction works had been completed, and five months later the anticipated full complement of 750 workers had been achieved.

The Whitecrook site used was the former JBLB site at Stanford Street, which comprised two large sheds and a stockyard. In total there was 426,500 square feet of space available, 120,000 square feet of which was covered. Between them, the sheds contained five fabrication bays. At their peak these bays were producing 8,000 tons of fabrication annually. Here fabrications were manufactured to sub-assembly stage and, when complete, were hoisted by overhead cranes onto trailers for transporting to Rothesay Dock for final assembly and shipping. Because the loads were big and heavy, progress to the Dock was inevitably slow and a police escort was required. The two routes used were via Whitecrook Street, Cart

An aerial view of the Rothesay Dock showing a loading out barge, alongside the Plettac prefabricated sheds

Street and into Rothesay Dock by its western entrance, or via Whitecrook Street and Glasgow Road before turning into Dock Street and the eastern entrance to the Dock.

Situated beside the river, immediately to the east of the shipyard, Rothesay Dock was initially to be known as the Clydebank Dock. However, it was named Rothesay Dock after the Prince of Wales (who was also the Duke of Rothesay) who opened it. Completed in 1911 at a cost of £500,000, the Dock covered a total area of 76 acres, comprising an outer and inner basin, a power station, cranage and ancillary equipment. Overall, it had a combined water area of over 19 acres, in addition to 1,847 yards of quayside. The entrance to the outer dock was 200 feet wide and the depth of water at ordinary tides was in excess of thirty-five feet. Railway sidings, which had been laid down by the Caledonian Railway Company, led directly into the Dock area. In 1966, Rothesay Dock became the responsibility of the newly-formed Clydeport.

Although originally built for the import of iron ore and the export of coal, with its excellent deep water frontage of 366 metres, a deep-water jetty, and a wide dock entrance, the Dock was easily capable of coping with the massive barges needed to handle fabrications

A North Sea fabrication being manoeuvred onto a loading out barge at the nearby Foster Wheeler yard in Dumbarton: the technique used at Rothesay Dock was exactly the same

of up to 2,000 tons in weight. However, since the site comprised soft ground, steps had to be taken to prepare the foundations within the Dock upon which the modules would rest - and thus avoid the loads sinking into the ground. This 'pad' was achieved by laying a mixture of concrete and metal beams on the ground. Site fabrications being assembled at the Dock were to be protected from the weather by two translucent Plettac Weatherall buildings, designed to give all-round daylight and a warm dry interior, thus allowing employees to work in all conditions. In addition, the roof sections could be increased, decreased, or removed, as necessary. In essence, the system was designed so that the dimensions could be altered to suit variable module sizes.

In early 1976 JBE Offshore's first fabrication, a 24-ton flare boom, was loaded onto the cargo vessel, *St. Kentigern*, at Rothesay Dock for shipping out to Holland. At that time the company was also completing modules ordered for the Dunlin and Brent fields, while others for Phillips and Chevron were in the process of construction. Preparations were also underway for the first completed module - a monster of between 400 and 600 tons built for Phillips Petroleum - to be shipped out. At this time the order book contained £10m worth of contracts, which included utilities modules, drill support modules, wellhead modules, and power generation and switchgear modules for the Phillips Petroleum Company's Eldfisk field; a sub-Main Power Generation Module, Water Injection Module, two Process Modules, Flare Boom and Crane Pedestal for Shell UK Exploration & Production Limited's Brent 'C' field; and an Electrical Module, Generation Module, Wellhead Module and

An aerial view of the Chevron Ninian Central platform. Three JBE-built Frame 5 gas turbines can be seen to the right of the heli-deck

Workshop/Control Module for the Chevron Petroleum (UK) Limited's Ninian field. Further work carried out for Chevron (sub-contracted to JBE Offshore by Cleveland Bridge) included prefabricated plate girder and node sections for the Ninian (Southern) field. Twenty-seven piping packages were also supplied for Shell Exploration & Production Company's Brent 'C' field.

Since the moving, and subsequent loading, of the fabrications was an extremely difficult and dangerous operation, sophisticated and varied lifting equipment was required. Within the Whitecrook fabrication sheds this included a Rol-Air system capable of moving twenty-five ton weights. At the Dock a Kramo-Montage jacking system was used, in addition to a Manitowoc 4100W strut jib crane (the tallest on Clydeside at the time) with a capacity to lift 200 tons. Modules were pushed into position by four bogies, which were coated with a low friction lubrication, each with jacks. The first critical factor in this operation was the tide on the River Clyde: the loading required to be done three hours before the high water mark, and thereafter completed within four hours. Various suitable dates were pencilled in where the necessary conditions would be met. Barges were strengthened and stabilised to ensure that the weight of the module being loaded was evenly balanced. To ensure stability, water was pumped into compartments within each barge using thirty pumps, operated from a command station situated on the Dock and controlled by JBE Offshore personnel. Once aboard the barge, the modules were temporarily jacked up to allow the bogies and tracks to be removed. Thereafter, the modules could be securely fastened to the deck of the barge, and the ballast of the barge then adjusted, so that the barge could be towed safely to the oil platform.

While JBE Offshore was beginning to establish itself during the mid-1970s, the IGT Division of JBE also secured a number of important North Sea contracts. These were for Frame 5 gas turbines for Occidental's Claymore field, Chevron's Ninian field, and Phillips Petroleum's Ekofisk Central and South fields.

Despite its successes, in 1977 JBE was obliged to face up to the probable closure of the ailing JBE Offshore Limited facility. Although it had had a promising start and the sales team had worked hard to generate new orders, in common with other UK module builders, it found sufficient work simply wasn't forthcoming and the facility was losing money. On 31 March 1977 therefore all JBE Offshore employees received official notification of possible impending redundancies and, shortly afterwards (on 1 July), over one hundred employees were made redundant. The company retained the remaining 284 employees, although there was in fact only sufficient work for fifty men. This was done partly to enable the company to take on any new work if and when it became available. However, the following year Rothesay Dock and Whitecrook Works were placed on a 'care and maintenance' basis. Despite the excellence of the facility at Clydebank, the down turn in demand for North Sea offshore work had now left the management with no other option but to close JBE Offshore. As there had been previous redundancies and rumours of closure, the final redundancies were accepted by the workforce with weary resignation. Since the company had been established as a separate entity, the men who were paid off (some of whom had transferred across from JBE), were not automatically transferred back to JBE but, instead, either went to other yards in search of work, or were obliged to re-apply for work within JBE. Notwithstanding its all too brief existence, JBE Offshore had, in the face of very difficult trading conditions, managed to secure orders for fifteen modules, twenty-seven piping packages, one flare boom, two crane pedestals, and sundry other fabrications, with a total value of over £16m.

---

i *JB News* (1978), April.
ii *JB News* (1978), April.
iii *JB Newsletter* (1971), Winter.
iv *JB Newsletter* (1971), Winter.
v *JB Newsletter* (1971), Winter.
vi *Clydebank Press* (1975), 31 January, p3.
vii *JB Newsletter* (1974), Winter.

6 JBE: The Company in the late 1970s

Setting up JBE Gas Turbines Limited
An increase in IGT's workload was one of the factors which led, in April 1975, to the formation of a subsidiary, JBE Gas Turbines Limited (JBEGT). This left the main Clydebank JBE Board with responsibility for corporate and administrative functions, together with some general engineering operations. This new subsidiary was established in recognition of the rapid growth and future potential of the IGT Division, and to enable it to undertake a comprehensive turnkey role. Although almost in every respect a 'stand alone' company, it utilised the Engine Works machinery and test bay facilities. Its Chairman was John Staniforth and its Managing Director, Bill Connell (who was also by then the Assistant Managing Director of JBE). John R. Mayhew-Sanders and Graham Strachan were both non-executive directors. Management included Alaister Forsyth (Director of Operations), Jim Turner (Director of Planning and Services), Harry Crawford (responsible for liaison with the Manufacturing Director, Bill Davie) and Allan Gormly (Director of Financial Services).

With the formation of two new subsidiary companies (JBE Offshore Limited and JBEGT), Graham Strachan's title was changed to that of Group Managing Director. A further, more minor, reorganisation was also carried through at this time: the Purchasing Department (by now responsible for co-ordinating purchases in excess of £20m each year), headed by Allan Gormly, was elevated to Divisional level. In addition a new Department, known as the Product Development Department, was formed. It was the responsibility of Ian Broadley, who was charged with assessing the viability of new products whose manufacture would be compatible with existing operations.

Looking back on JBE's first ten years
On 1 October 1976, with its order book at an all-time high, JBE celebrated its tenth anniversary with the launch of an anniversary brochure and a month long series of events to which employees and their families and friends, and business associates were invited. Notwithstanding a somewhat ominous start, with the failure of the steam turbines installed by JBE in the *QE2*, the decade had, in general been one where the company had tasted success after success. By the end of their first ten years a total of 250 gas turbines and associated equipment, worth a staggering £200m pounds, had been manufactured at Clydebank.

JBE was now run by a main Board comprising John Staniforth (Chairman), John R. Mayhew-Sanders (Deputy Chairman), Graham Strachan (Group Managing Director), Bill Connell (Assistant Managing Director), Lord Glenkinglas, Allan Gormly, Bill Davie, Jim Turner, Jim Dickson and Donald Macleod (Secretary).

Overall, JBE had seen considerable growth. The company's turnover had dramatically risen from a half-year figure of £1.1m in 1967, to over £31m in the year ending 31 March 1976. The full value of the North Sea work alone (modules and other fabrications, as well as gas turbines) had amounted to over £35m. Over the period, £8m of capital investment had been approved. Although this only amounted to approximately 16 per cent of turnover, in July 1976 the parent company approved a £2.4m modernisation and re-tooling programme.

Employment had more than doubled, from a workforce numbering 1,100 in 1966 to over

A pipe band at Rothesay Dock during Open Day celebrations, 9 October 1976

Family and friends in the Engine Works during Open Day, 9 October 1976

2,000 in 1976. Demarcation and other Union issues, however, had bedevilled JBE in the earlier years. Despite this, in 1976 Bill Davie, Manufacturing Director, praised not only the traditional skills and motivation of his workforce, but the discipline of the Unions in the company's formative years.

The success of the company was also reflected in the many awards it had won. The two Manufacturing Associate of the Year Awards had placed JBE foremost among the various MAs, however, undoubtedly the most significant awards were the four Queens Awards for Export Achievement (won in 1970, 1971, 1972 and 1974). Each of these awards was well-deserved, as exports had risen from £3m in 1968 to over £100m in 1974. Furthermore, the

The presentation of JBE's second Queens Award to JBE Chairman, John Staniforth (on the right) by Lord Lieutenant Robert Arbuthnott, 1971

The platform party at the presentation of JBE's third Queens Award, 1972

winning of the first three Awards over consecutive years was almost unique within the industry. In addition, in 1972 a new Queens Award for Technological Achievement had been won for the work undertaken by JBE on the Thistle 'A' North Sea oil platform.

Of all its undoubted achievements during that first ten years, however, perhaps the most remarkable of all was the transformation from an old-fashioned traditional engineering operation to an assembly line establishment, without any major mishaps. JBE had become a successful and significant international power contractor with a seemingly 'Midas' touch that guided it through potential minefields. Many lessons had been learned, much had been achieved, and a rapidly growing reputation enhanced. Would the next ten years bring more of the same, or would an ever competitive and sophisticated market create difficulties for this relative newcomer?

... and looking to the present

Unfortunately, for the parent company John Brown & Company Limited the late 1970s were to be undoubtedly one of the most difficult periods it had ever experienced. This was despite better than expected performance from some of its Divisions, and modest increases in annual pre-tax profits. In fact, the parent company was, overall, in a poor financial state, brought about by the fluctuating performances of the various Divisions, and the acquisition of various companies. Some of these acquisitions (notably machine tools and plastics) had proved to be unwise, while even core businesses such as the gas turbine and construction sectors were struggling. The situation was worsened by the high cost of sterling.

The general financial problems bedevilling the Group first became apparent in November 1978, when the parent company made it known that it was seeking to raise an additional £16m of capital to strengthen liquid reserves, and finance continuing investment and further acquisitions. To raise this money the then incoming Group Chairman, John Mayhew-Sanders, initiated a rights issue. Following its success, and boosted by a better than forecasted financial year end performance, the parent company's shares jumped 16p in January 1979.[i] This was due to a better than expected performance from JBE, CJB and the trailor makers, Craven Tasker. However, the continuing poor performance of the Machine Tool and Plastics Divisions continued to trouble the Group. Their response was to announce a twenty-five per cent cut in overall capacity, some redundancies, and the closure of the Wickman Lang plant in Johnstone, Renfrewshire. Notwithstanding, the Group's financial difficulties, John Mayhew-Sanders remained characteristically optimistic. He talked about John Brown & Company acquiring a "fourth arm",[ii] rather than the likely loss of a company such as JBE to their competitors. This optimism had its basis in improvements in the financial position, a £30m cash reserve and the £16m raised through the rights issue. And for JBE, it was business as usual immediately after its tenth anniversary celebrations. The company saw record outputs: in the twelve months to 1 April 1977, fifty gas turbines had been manufactured, tested and shipped out - easily beating the previous best of thirty-eight.

There were changes in key personnel. In 1977 JBE Chairman, John Staniforth (a staunch supporter of the Clydebank management) retired, being replaced by the Deputy Chairman, John Mayhew-Sanders. Shortly afterwards, Allan Gormly (Financial Director at Clydebank since 1970) was promoted to the London office, and Raymond McCabe took over his role. The following year, a restructuring of JBEGT resulted in the promotion of Alaister Forsyth to Director and General Manager of the Operations Group, and the appointment of four new Directors. Similarly, a re-organisation of the Manufacturing Division saw JBE Offshore Director James Dickson appointed to the post of Group Manufacturing Director, with Bill Davie appointed Group Director of Personnel.

This period also saw the expansion and modernisation of the Clydebank gas turbine facility. A £10m modernisation in 1978 was part of a continuing process of change - it immediately followed a relatively modest modernisation which had commenced in 1976. On that occasion the expenditure of £2.4m, which had been partly provided through a government Accelerated Investments Projects scheme, had mostly gone towards providing new machinery for Bay 9 and the Fabrication Works. Approximately £365,000 was also

The Test Bay in the Engine Works

utilised to upgrade and extend the test facilities (the latter being necessary to cope with the large numbers of new orders for turbines). It included the re-siting of the No.1 test stand into Bay 12, the formation of a new No.4 test stand, and the installation of an acoustic wall between Bays 11 and 12. The modernisation in 1978 included the refurbishment of existing machinery and an upgrading of the cranage facility.

Equally significant was the amalgamation of the Installation, Services and Spares Departments to form a new Customer Services Division (CSD). This new Division, headed by Mike Pell (recruited from sister company CJB), was set up to provide a comprehensive support service for JBE's customers. The first fruits of this initiative were demonstrated in late 1979 when JBE were awarded their largest ever spare parts contract. The order, worth several million pounds, was placed by Russian trading partners Machinoimport and covered the supply of spare parts for all GE-designed gas turbines in Russia.

In the early 1970s the original MA Agreement was extended, and the range of gas turbine models built at Clydebank was expanded. There was a growing awareness of the need to progress from waste heat recovery and desalination applications to the new combined cycle units with their higher fuel efficiencies and quicker delivery times. The latter necessitated the manufacture of the more advanced 35mw Frame 6 unit and the much larger Frame 9 unit: at the time (in 1974) the largest of its size in the world.

In 1978, in order to supplement their existing range of models, JBE signed a ten-year MA Agreement with GE to enable the company to package and sell the new GE LM2500 gas turbine. The recommendation to introduce this new lightweight and compact model came from the recently formed Product Development Department. However, despite its obvious advantages (which included an ability to operate without on-site personnel - an advantage in remote locations), no firm orders were ever received for this turbine.

In the winter of 1978, *JBE's Big Un* - a 90mw single shaft Frame 9 gas turbine - was unveiled.[iii] This turbine, specifically designed for the 50 cycle market, was basically a scaled up version of the existing Frame 7, but twice its size. As there was insufficient space at Clydebank to build these units, the first five (destined for the Dubal Aluminium Company smelter) were built in the former Alexander Stephen's shipyard at Linthouse, Govan. Stephen & Sons had been shipbuilders, engine builders and repairers that had fallen on hard times in the 1960s, and eventually been absorbed into UCS. In 1977, JBE negotiated a three-year lease for the use of two Engine Works bays for the construction of the new Frame 9 turbines. Later a second lease was taken out for additional bays to enable more Frame 9s to be built in the Works. Ultimately the entire yard, comprising ten acres, was acquired. In addition to temporarily resolving the space problem, the Stephen's yard had the additional bonus of being in close proximity to the King George V Dock.

In early May 1979, the first of the new Frame 9 gas turbines left the old Stephen's Yard. The responsibility for the transport of this 220-ton load (the heaviest single load that had ever been handled by the Shipping Department) fell to Douglas McCaw. While no difficulties were experienced by the lorry on the way to King George V Dock, once the Dock was reached several major problems were encountered! Firstly, the turbine had to remain on the trailer on the quayside, as it was feared that a tunnel underneath the Dock complex might

JBE at the Dubal Aluminium Smelter

collapse from the weight of the Frame 9 unit if it was allowed to rest upon it. Secondly, it was found that the cranes on board the freighter (*the Strathearl*) which was to transport the turbine to Dubai were inadequate, and the use of additional spreader bars was necessary. A quick call had to be made to the JBE Fabrication Works at Clydebank, which constructed the necessary lifting gear in less than three hours! When the load was eventually lifted onto the vessel (it took seven attempts), a "great cheer went up from the dock-side".[iv] The additional lifting gear prepared by the Fabrication Works was stowed away on the ship for re-use when the unit was being off-loaded in Dubai. It was then brought back to Clydebank and used again when a further four Frame 9 units were being shipped out to Dubai.

Other contracts won in the late 1970s were two from the Electric Power Corporation of Burma for installations at Rangoon and Mann. These contracts, worth just over £10m, were for packaged power plants and associated equipment. Gas turbines were also supplied to the Dubai Natural Gas's Jebel Ali plant, and BP's oil refinery extension in Holland, the latter being JBE's first Dutch order.

Tough Times
In mid-1979, the parent company John Brown & Company Limited (described in a contemporary magazine article as a "favourite son"[v] of the Stock Exchange) surprised city analysts with the announcement of record profits of £28.2m for the financial year ending 31 March. These profits, up from £23m in the previous financial year, caused shares to jump by 14p and were the result of better than expected profits from several of the Divisions. This was especially true of JBE, where profits had increased from £7.47m to £10.13m on a turnover up from £71.17m to £80.17m. Ironically, these figures were achieved despite the production of gas turbines being down by a third from the record-breaking fifty of the previous year. However, despite these record results, later that year (with the Board desperately seeking to reduce their sizeable debt mountain), John Mayhew-Sanders was obliged to issue a warning of difficult times in the coming years. By March 1980 the seriousness of the financial situation was spelt out to all employees with the circulation of the interim *Annual Report*. This showed a collapse in profits from £28.2m to £18m.

In January 1981 the parent company's financial problems worsened. In the middle of a world-wide recession, and still suffering from the high cost of sterling, the parent company issued an interim statement indicating that profits were likely to fall by half from the record £28.2m of two years previously. For the twelve months to 31 March 1981 John Mayhew-Sanders intimated that, despite sales of £700m, profits could be as low as £12m (they were ultimately £14m). This last announcement caused some downward movement in the share price, and was followed by the loss of approximately 4,000 jobs throughout the Group (including 700 at Clydebank), and the closure of eight plants by the following March. The Group's swing from profit to loss was largely attributed to poor performance by JBE (a major part of the parent company). However, after struggling to win new orders, JBE's performance improved and profits increased. Ironically, however, in the short term, this further depleted the already fragile Group reserves, as they had to set aside cash guarantees to ensure the successful completion of the JBE contracts.

Six hundred redundancies at Clydebank in September 1979, and, shortly afterwards, a streamlining of top tier management, had been justified by Graham Strachan as being necessary to slim down the work force to adapt, not only to the fall in demand for gas turbines (caused by the high cost of fuel), but an increasing demand for larger and more efficient units.

The management changes had become clear on 22 October 1979, when the separate management structure set up for JBEGT in 1975 was abandoned, and JBEGT absorbed back into JBE (Clydebank) Limited to operate as one integrated unit. Within this unit, a new management structure of four main Groups (all reporting directly to the JBE Group Managing Director, Graham Strachan) was set up. The Groups, each of which was headed by a Director, comprised Manufacturing and Personnel (Jim Dickson), Operations (Alaister Forsyth), Financial and Management Services (Raymond McCabe) and Sales, Marketing & Development (Brian Nicholls). In the main, senior management was little affected by this re-organisation, except for Jim Turner, who relinquished his position as Director of Management Services in favour of Raymond McCabe, and was retained for special assignment work (reporting direct to Graham Strachan). Other minor personnel changes included the promotion of Hugh Stevenson (who became responsible for the Management Services section within Raymond McCabe's Financial and Management Services Group) and Bill Davie taking responsibility for the Personnel Department, which was brought into Jim Dickson's Manufacturing & Personnel Directorate.

Bill Connell - a key figure in JBE's development

Perhaps the most significant personnel change, however, was Bill Connell relinquishing his executive positions with JBE and JBEGT on 1 November 1979, to take up the post of Head of Group Product Planning & Market Development in London (reporting directly to the Group Chairman, John Mayhew-Sanders). Bill had been one of the key architects in JBE's early development, and had been largely responsible for the development of the IGT Division. Later, in 1984, he left the Group and took up the position of Sales Director Middle & Far East with rivals Hawker Siddeley Power Engineering, where he remained until his retirement in 1988.

In early 1980 Jim Turner, another company stalwart from the early years also retired. A tireless worker,[vi] Jim had joined the company in 1964 as Engineering Sales Manager and was

Presentation to Jim Turner on his retirement

– 56 –

JBE Sales Director John Barlow with the Duke of Kent, at the 1979 China Energy Show

one of the original members of the senior management team at the formation of JBE in 1966. Other changes in senior management were occasioned by the resignations of Jim Dickson (Group Manufacturing Director) who was replaced by Harry Crawford, and Bill Davie (Group Personnel Director). John Barlow was also appointed Sales Director.

The changing market led to the existing Gas Turbine Model Policy being reviewed. A decision was made to scale down production of the basic Frame 5 model after 1981, concentrating instead on the new Frame 6 and Frame 9 models. Another consequence of the review was the formation of the Masaood John Brown Gulf Service Centre. It was announced at the first ever Middle East gas turbine show (held in Bahrain in 1979), where JBE also unveiled their latest installation: the much acclaimed 128mw Scotstag combined cycle plant.

Notwithstanding the lack of orders throughout the latter part of 1979, Graham Strachan remained cautiously optimistic that JBE would return to profit in the foreseeable future. However, despite a steadier market for gas turbine contracts, his efforts to seek further orders were hampered by the difficult trading position and global political issues. More importantly, the weakness of the American dollar, while seemingly benefiting UK firms, led to a downturn in demand for gas turbines for the American domestic market, forcing companies such as GE to seek new orders from JBE's traditional markets. The securing of five new orders, announced on 19 February 1980, did, however, guarantee full employment for the workforce in the immediate future.

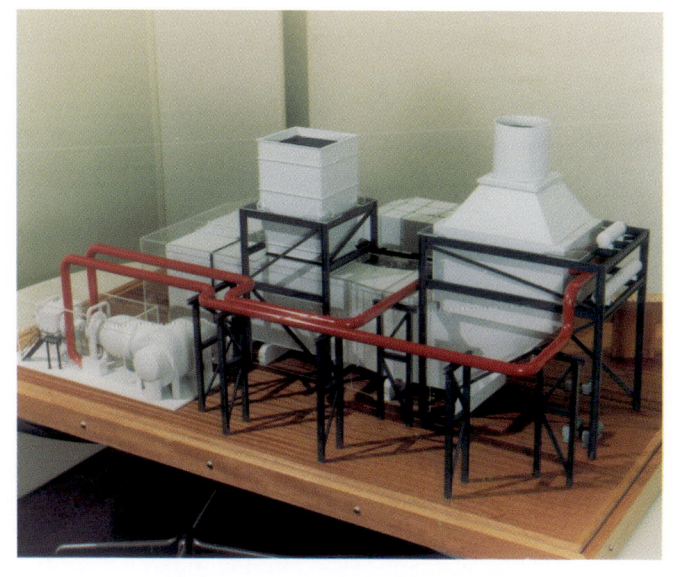

How it worked: the Scotstag system

These orders included two new North Sea contracts from Matthew Hall Engineering Limited (on behalf of the BP Magnus Development Project) for three 25mw Frame 5 gas turbine generating sets and one 10mw Frame 3 gas turbine generating set for Conoco UK for their Immingham Refinery on Humberside. As main contractor on the Matthew Hall/BP project, the parent company was responsible for the design, engineering and installation of the 40,000 ton Magnus oil platform, which, at that time, was not only the deepest and most northerly oil platform in the North Sea, but also the world's heaviest one piece structure. In 1981 the Clydebank-built gas turbines equipped to supply all the power required by the BP Magnus field were shipped out, and the entire contract was completed in 1982.

The other orders at this time were repeat orders, attributed not only to competitive cost and delivery factors, but the maintenance of good relations with existing customers. These included an order for five 25mw Frame 5 gas turbine generating sets from consulting engineers, Ewbank & Partners, for the Aluminium Bahrain Power Station, bringing the total gas turbines now supplied to this power station to twenty-four. Further orders won at this time included: a £35m contract by the Arabian Gulf Exploration Company (AGECO) of Libya for the supply and installation of two Frame 5 gas turbine power plants to power oil pumping plant at the Messa oil field some 300 miles west of Tripoli; three 25mw Frame 5 gas turbines and two Waste Heat Recovery Boilers for the Electric Power Corporation of Burma, for sites 200 miles north of Rangoon; an £8m order for three Frame 5 gas turbine generating sets placed by the Ceylon Electricity Board; and a £1.6m order placed by the Grand Bahamas Development Company for the Freeport Power Company. Taken together, these new orders provided a reasonable forward order book but, more importantly, substantially reduced the stock of unsold units. However, despite the magnitude of these orders (cumulatively worth over £21m), Strachan cautioned that 1980 could turn out to be another difficult year. Indeed, as he had anticipated, 1980 proved to be the grimmest year in the Company's history to date, with morale at an all time low. Like their competitors, JBE had to export to survive, but by the end of the year, with no new orders, JBE was forced to issue redundancy notices to a further seventy-five Clydebank workers to correct an imbalance of skills. In the event, these redundancy notices were withdrawn at the last minute when, during the Christmas holiday period, the company secured four contracts worth £60m for installations in Brunei, India, Iraq and Oman. These much needed contracts provided fifteen months of full employment for the workforce. However, although it then

Magnus North Sea oil platform

Harold Wilson, British Prime Minister, presents Jim Liddell, JBE Safety Manager, with a British Safety Council award

Bill Connell (on the left) and Jim McDowell (on the right) with Sir Keith Joseph, Minister of Trade and Industry, at the presentation of the 1979 National Marketing Award

seemed likely that the 1981-82 financial year figures should show a marked swing from loss to profit, John Mayhew-Sanders cautioned that, in the longer term, the future of Clydebank's 1,600 strong workforce would depend on their winning further orders and adopting a sensible approach to wage claim demands.

Despite all of these difficulties, JBE had gained many awards in the late 1970s and early 1980s, including an Institute of Marketing National Marketing award, a Confederation of British Industries Ideas at Work award, and (in 1980) a fifth consecutive award from the British Safety Council.

In the early 1980s a better understanding of the growing international nature of the power engineering business led to further changes. Thus in April 1980, an ostensibly minor, but in many ways significant, change occurred when the Clydebank subsidiary's name was changed from JBE (Clydebank) Limited to simply JBE Limited. Understandably, omitting Clydebank from the title caused some soul-searching in a local community proud of its shipbuilding heritage. There were also several major developments, reflecting concern about the rather haphazard layout of the Clydebank facility and more especially about the 'face' it presented to the many foreign clients visiting the factory to view work in progress. This was particularly so within the former Engine Works. Here, the existing twelve Bays were utilised in as practical a way as possible, but it was not possible to achieve a proper flow of work as befitted what was, essentially, an assembly line type of operation. Gas turbines, for example, were largely assembled in Bay One, with their various assemblies and casings manufactured in adjoining Bays. Before final assembly, however, the turbines had to be transported on bogies the length of the Engine Works to Bay Twelve, where they were rigorously tested before being returned to Bay One for final assembly. The Fabrication Works, where various sub-assemblies were manufactured, was likewise some distance from the Engine Works Bays and so again components had to be transported.

Another pressing problem was the administration accommodation that, over the years, had become somewhat of a rabbit's warren of offices, some of which were leased from UIE who shared the site. Throughout the 1970s, this matter had exercised the minds of the Clydebank

Above: The demolition of the tenements on Glasgow Road, in 1978
Left: Clydebank Terrace, Glasgow Road, Clydebank, later site of the new JBE administration block
Reproduced courtesy of West Dunbartonshire Libraries

Board. In March 1973, a piece of ground owned by JBE, fronting Dumbarton Road (west of the JBE entrance) was considered for a new headquarters building. A brief was prepared by Anthony Masters & Associates and submitted the following month.

However, the long and narrow nature of the site posed architectural problems. In addition, its position on Dumbarton Road would have resulted in high noise levels. Accordingly, this proposal was not proceeded with. However, in 1979 the then Financial Director, Raymond McCabe, finally determined to resolve the office accommodation problem. Raymond McCabe had been much impressed with new District Council Offices which had just been built in Rosebery Place, Clydebank, by Bison of Falkirk, and so requested the company to build a similar one for JBE. The new administration block was opened in 1982 at a cost of £1.25m. Other improvements at that time included a £200,000 refurbishment of the former Sheet Iron Shop (to provide office and storage accommodation for the restructured CSD section of Power Systems) and the re-roofing of Bay Twelve.

JBE Sales Manager, Brian Nicholls (second from left) at the Empressa Provincial de Energia Power Station in Argentina

The scarcity of orders for most of 1980 and the resultant loss of £1.2m in the financial year ending 1981, changed when £235m worth of contracts were won by JBE in 1981. One of the new orders announced in May 1981 was a contract from Argentina. This contract, won in the face of fierce international competition, was worth £25m and involved the conversion of two existing power stations for combined cycle operation. JBE's part was to supply two Frame 5 gas turbines to Empressa Provincial de Energia de Cordoba. These were then converted to more efficient and cost-saving combined cycle units by adding Waste Heat Recovery Boilers (WHRBs) and steam turbo alternator sets. The conflict arising from the Argentinian claim of sovereignty over the Falkland Islands, and the subsequent bad blood between Britain and Argentina forced JBE to withdraw from this contract before the work was finished. Despite insurance cover by the Export Credits Guarantee Department (ECGD), JBE suffered a loss. As will be seen in the next chapter, it would not be the first time that JBE found itself in the middle of an international dispute.

---

i   This saw profits increase from a little over £23m to around £28m in the financial year ending March 1978.
ii *Glasgow Herald* (1979), 27 January, p11.
iii *JB News* (1978), Winter.
iv *JB News* (1979), April/May.
v *Chemical Age International* (1979), July.
vi *JB News* (1980), March.

7   Three projects memorable for the wrong reasons

Bani Yas

If 1980 was a bleak year for JBE, it was as nothing compared to the following two years, when the company was almost brought to its knees by a series of unconnected events. The first of these was self-inflicted and was brought about by the almost desperate need to break into the new Frame 6 market in order to get a financial return on the units then under construction. The manufacture of the first Frame 6s began in 1980, but despite some encouraging enquiries, no firm orders were secured until 1981, when two were received for installations in Bani Yas and Bouganville. In August that year, in the face of fierce international competition, JBE signed a contract worth almost £28m with the Ministry of Water and Electricity (WED) in Abu Dhabi to build a 100mw power station at Bani Yas, and upgrade existing facilities at Abu Dhabi town's Power Station and the Al Ain Power Station. As JBE had previously successfully undertaken work for this client (including, in 1976, the supply of Frame 5 units for the Al Ain Power Station), there was no reason to suspect that the new contract would not run smoothly. Sadly, it turned out to be a disastrous contract that was not completed on schedule, and ultimately cost the company almost £20m in penalties and additional costs.

The Bani Yas Power Station. Although a loss-making project, the completed power station was generally considered to be an outstanding engineering achievement

The contract was secured with the assistance of JBE's local agents, Mohammed Bin Masaood & Sons. Like other UK companies operating in foreign markets JBE found it necessary, and sometimes obligatory, to appoint a local agent to assist in establishing contacts, smoothing contract negotiations, and advising on local laws and customs. JBE had worked informally for many years with the Masaood Brothers in the Middle East. In 1979 it was decided to formalise this relationship, and this led to the formation of Masaood John

Brown Limited, a joint venture company providing after sales services, which became highly successful.

The Bani Yas contract required that four Frame 6 gas turbines be supplied and commissioned, and the contract completed, by July 1982. In October 1981, when the contract was first announced, it was seen as highly significant for JBE, since it not only provided much needed work, but allowed them an entry into the Frame 6 market. Ironically, given the ultimate outcome, Brian Nicholls (JBE's Sales & Marketing Director at that time) paid tribute to the foresight of the development team that encouraged JBE "to take the lead on Frame 6's".[i]

The contract and the tender documents were prepared by German consultants, Lahmeyer International, who were appointed by WED to oversee the contract. Crucially, the contract did not include an exclusion clause and the consultants were able to exploit (to their client's advantage) any vagueness in the contract documents, and in so doing seriously delayed the contract. It led to speculation that the consultants had expected to be dealing with another contractor and that the power station layout and specification were based largely on that other contractor's practices and proposals. In addition, WED's preference for, and Lahmeyer's insistence on, using German suppliers meant that a tendering process, which should have taken weeks to complete, in fact took months. As JBE's contract price had been based on use of their traditional suppliers there was limited scope for using more expensive vendors. Further problems (and delays) occurred at the design stage, as the consultants insisted on receiving detailed plant design information before they would approve related civil engineering design details. Further, it soon became apparent that JBE's tender price was impossibly low if the demands of the consultants were to be met.

In August 1982, with the work incomplete, Lahmeyer advised JBE that they proposed to recover the standard 10 per cent penalty from future invoices (amounting to some £1.4m) because of JBE's failure to achieve the agreed completion dates: no further invoices would be paid until the value of future invoices exceeded the penalty amount. The immediate result was that there was no cash income from the project. Further penalties were incurred and numerous personnel were drafted in to attempt to resolve the many problems and to mediate in the protracted disputes with the client and the German consultants. It was not until 1987 that the final completion certificates were issued. In retrospect, the Bani Yas contract proved to be the most disastrous in the Company's history up till then. Indeed, but for the steady annual profits made at that time by JBE from other major contracts, it could have threatened JBE's very existence. It was the first contract on which JBE incurred substantial penalties. Ironically, it was later discovered that JBE's original tender price, together with the contract loss, had more or less matched the next lowest tender of approximately £40m. Notwithstanding the financial problems, the Bani Yas Power Station was by all accounts one of the most sophisticated in the Middle East, and was a fine engineering achievement for JBE.

Iraq

An Iraqi contract secured during the Iran-Iraq war proved to be a very risky venture which could have cost the lives of some of the workers on site. JBE, having previously supplied four Frame 5 units for a consortium comprising Thyssen-Lummus and the Iraq National Refinery, and knowing that Iranian forces had damaged Iraqi power stations and heavy plant, saw an

Gas Turbine No.336 at Aqaba, 1981

opportunity for further, much needed, orders. Consequently, JBE entered into negotiations with Iraqi officials for the supply of replacement gas turbines which Clydebank had in stock. Following these talks, JBE were invited to send a negotiating team to Baghdad. Accordingly, at the beginning of December 1980, a small team of six headed by Alaister Forsyth left for Iraq. Verbal agreement was reached on New Year's Eve, the resultant letter of intent signed on 1 January 1981, and finally the contract on 28th January.

The risky nature of the Iraqi contracts was later recalled by Hugh McGinty, the JBE Senior Shipping Officer in Iraq, who was responsible for ensuring that all incoming equipment was cleared through the port of Aqaba, and safely transported by road to the power station at Kirkuk in Northern Iraq. To get to Baghdad, JBE employees were required to take an Iraqi Airways late night flight from Amman in Jordan, which picked up a fighter escort at the Iraqi border. Once in Baghdad, they were accommodated in a six bedroom property which, although substantial, was in fact little more than a transit camp - being used both as an arrival and departure point for JBE personnel coming into and leaving Iraq, and as a place where men on site could periodically come to for some respite. Thus, there was rarely a time when a complete night's rest was possible! One night a colleague, Bill Isbister, had gone to the airport to pick up one of the arriving engineers, and was caught up in an air raid on the airport! On another occasion, at the height of the conflict, several JBE employees working near Basra on the Thyssen-Lummus contract, narrowly escaped injury when their canteen was hit by a stray bomb from an Iranian fighter jet. Together with forty-five other foreign nationals (including women and children), they decided to leave the site and make a dash for the Kuwaiti border. Commandeering a truck, they drove to the border, but were refused passage because, in their hurry to leave, they had left behind their passports and exit visas!

Fortunately, two Americans in the party volunteered to return for the passports and visas and, after hours of delay, they were all allowed to proceed.

JBE and the Russian Pipeline Embargo

Undeniably the most dramatic event in the company's history was the embargo on the export of American technology to Russia announced by US President Ronald Reagan in October

Presentation of a gas turbine model to a Soviet official by JBE installation engineer, John Turner, during the Urengoy pipeline works

A compressor station on the Urengoy pipeline

1981. This had serious implications for JBE who, following a major sales drive in Russia in early 1979, had secured (in addition to a £5m order from Machinoimport for one Frame 3 mechanical drive gas turbine and spare parts) a share of a massive pipeline order worth £104m. It was this contract (easily JBE's largest to date) that sucked JBE, their fellow MAs in France and Germany, and their respective governments into a major trade dispute between the USSR and the USA.

This new pipeline contract was concluded in September 1981 with Machinoimport partners, MAB-Creusot-Loire, and was for twenty-one Frame 5 two shaft mechanical drive gas turbines and spare parts for seven compressor stations to drive natural gas along a new pipeline.

The background to this project was the Soviet government's intention to construct a major 3,500 mile long new pipeline between Urengoy and Uzhgorod, to carry 35bn cubic feet of natural gas annually from Siberia. When negotiations began with Machinoimport, it appeared that two British companies could be in the running to supply some of the 125 gas turbines needed to drive gas through the new pipeline. These were Rolls Royce, who manufactured a lighter aero-derivative turbine, and JBE, who built the heavy-duty GE model. Ultimately, the GE-designed gas turbine was chosen and the consortium consisting of AEG-Kanis of Germany, JBE, and Nuovo Pignone of Italy, secured the contract. Inevitably, this coup received much favourable media coverage. With £180m of exports already in their order book, it guaranteed work for the 1,700 strong JBE workforce until late 1983.

Initially, all went well and the manufacture of the twenty-one JBE turbines commenced.

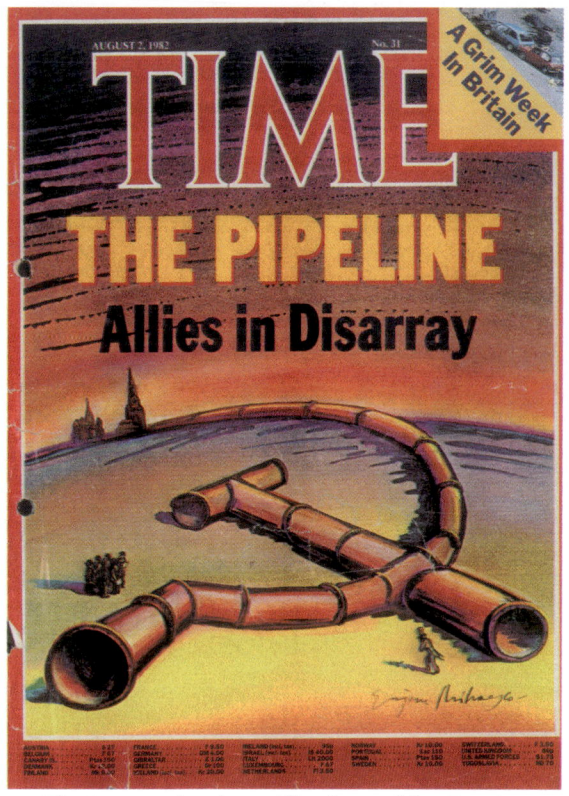

The international ramifications of the Russian Pipeline embargo headlined on the front cover of Time magazine in 1982
Reproduced courtesy of Getty Images

However, in late October 1981 (in response to the imposition of martial law, and the banning of the Solidarity movement, in Poland) President Reagan, imposed sanctions on the Soviet Union. These sanctions were expanded on 18 June 1982 to include equipment necessary for the extraction of oil and gas. Since the gas turbines under construction by JBE (and other MAs) contained rotors, stator blades and nozzles manufactured in America by GE, the embargo effectively meant that this contract could not be proceeded with.

The embargo left the consortium with a serious dilemma. On the one hand, a contract worth many millions of pounds would be lost, and the Soviet authorities were also threatening to invoke severe penalty clauses should there be any delay in fulfilling the contract. Furthermore, although it was thought that the John Brown group could survive the loss of this prestigious contract, there were fears that others in the consortium would not. On the other hand, failure to comply with the sanctions would lead to GE being unable to supply the fifteen further rotors required to complete the contract, and JBE being blacklisted by the American government, thus jeopardising future contracts.

Throughout the months of June and July, while JBE proceeded to manufacture the first six gas turbines using rotors supplied by GE before the sanctions were imposed, intense lobbying by Prime Minister Margaret Thatcher and her Ministers was taking place behind the scenes. By late July, however, and with no end to the dispute in sight, the British Trade Secretary, Lord Cuckfield instructed JBE to proceed with the shipment of the first gas turbines. The UK government's initiative was soon followed by the German, French and Italian governments. In late August 1982 therefore JBE prepared to be blacklisted by the US government, and transported the first six gas turbines to King George V Dock in Glasgow for loading onto the Soviet freighter, *Stakhanovets Yermolenko*. Simultaneously, at Le Havre three compressors manufactured by Dresser Industries (a French subsidiary of an American company) were being taken on board the French owned freighter, *Borodin*. The following month, the German firm AEG-Kanis also broke ranks and shipped out the first of their gas turbines to Russia.

At the beginning of September, as the *Stakhanovets Yermolenko* left the River Clyde en route to Leningrad, the threatened sanctions, in the form of a Temporary Denial Order, were imposed on JBE. This forbade the export of gas turbines to the USA by JBE. This was quickly followed by the imposition of similar sanctions on the other consortium partners. The John Brown board, on behalf of JBE, decided to take action through the US courts and accordingly appointed a Washington law firm to act on their behalf. Ultimately, however, the widespread defiance of the consortium partners, fiercely supported by their respective governments, obliged President Reagan to put forward a formula to resolve this major trade dispute. Sanctions were eventually dropped in early November 1982.

---

i *JB News* (1981), October.

8 Back from the Brink

The Hawker Siddeley Take-over Bid
The third major event to hit the company in the beginning of the 1980s came in December 1982 in the middle of the embargo crisis, when JBE was rocked by widespread speculation in the City and the media, that the parent company was threatened by a take-over bid on account of its poor trading position. Despite the announcement of a possible £9m loss, compared with profits of £14m the previous year, these rumours were denied by John Mayhew-Sanders. However, of the names being mooted, the favoured 'white knight' was Northern Engineering Industries (NEI). NEI was also in the power engineering business and, unlike John Brown, had an extremely healthy £180m market tag. On 5 January 1983, Graham Strachan dismissed these rumours in an internal memo, stating that the parent company, while still struggling financially, had sufficient cash reserves, and that no approach had been made to John Brown. There was further speculation in January 1983, this time regarding the future of John Mayhew-Sanders.

In reporting a half-year loss forecast of £9,400,000, John Mayhew-Sanders was forced to admit that all Divisions in the parent company were suffering from a down turn in demand, and that not even the very welcome JBE Russian pipeline order of 1981 would affect the overall performance. This news was not welcomed by the institutional shareholders and it was thought that there may be drastic changes within the parent company, including the removal of John Mayhew-Sanders. Shareholders were particularly angry at the expected loss of £10m by a recent American acquisition Leesona Plastics, together with the suspicion that the parent company had used the £25m raised from the 1981 share issue to acquire another loss-making American subsidiary, rather than strengthening its UK Divisions. On 6 February 1983, the parent company conceded that its debt problems could be resolved by the sale of JBE for £35m to NEI. In April 1983, with Graham Strachan and the Clydebank workforce still somewhat in the dark concerning these rumours, Clydebank MP, Hugh McCartney, met with John Mayhew-Sanders to clarify JBE's position. While a bid by NEI would have provided a short-term solution for John Brown, it would also have provided an opportunity for GE to terminate its Manufacturing Agreement with JBE, since NEI was a competitor of GE.

It soon emerged that the likely bidders for JBE were not in fact NEI, but GE and the UK engineering giant Hawker Siddeley. The latter were (like JBE) heavily involved in engineering but, unlike JBE, had the additional capability to manufacture generators, switchgears, and other engineering equipment necessary for the range of turnkey projects which JBE were increasingly being asked to tender for. Indeed, one of Hawker Siddeley's subsidiaries was the Brush Electrical Company Limited, who had been supplying generators to JBE since 1967. Its Managing Director (and a member of the Hawker Siddeley Board at the time of the proposed take-over) was John Durber. 'Mac' Durber was strongly in favour of this bid and, together with John Brown Director, Allan Gormly, came to Clydebank to address the workforce. Although the proposed bid for JBE received a favourable response from management and workers, it was ultimately not proceeded with, and was seen by some as a lost opportunity for JBE.

A New Team

In September 1983 the architect of JBE in its formative years, Graham Strachan, resigned. Coming shortly after the abortive take-over by Hawker Siddeley, and in advance of major redundancies at Clydebank, the shock resignation prompted speculation that he did not see eye to eye with the parent company's new Chairman, Sir John Cuckney. However, after thirty years at Clydebank (the last fifteen as Managing Director) Graham Strachan said it was simply a personal decision: he felt it was time to move on. He retained the position of non-executive Deputy Chairman until he eventually left the company. With the resignation of Graham Strachan, Raymond McCabe was appointed to be the new Managing Director.

By late 1983, the Group - at one time one of the major players in engineering in Britain - was, sadly, on the verge of bankruptcy. John Cuckney, therefore wasted no time in drawing up a corporate survival plan, designed to return the Group to profitability by financial year 1985-86. This plan, unveiled to impatient shareholders in January 1984, included an injection of £36m of fresh capital, £36m of assets to be written off, and provision for a major restructuring of the Group's operations, including the disposal of non-core activities. Within a year these drastic measures resulted in a modest recovery in the Group's

Raymond McCabe, Managing Director JBE 1983-1996

fortunes. For example, pre-tax losses had dropped to £5.6m, and bank borrowing (although still high in comparison with equity holdings of £40m) had been reduced to £109m. More importantly, some £15m of income had been raised by the disposal of loss-making assets, such as the US subsidiary machine tools company, Olofsson. Inevitably, and fuelled by speculation in the City, these disposals raised renewed fears about the future of JBE. Although Sir John ruled out any short-term divestments in August 1984, he conceded that JBE could still benefit from an association with another power generation group such as ASEA of Sweden, GEC or NEI.

Further developments promoted by the parent company and designed to further reduce costs and increase efficiency also impacted on the Clydebank operation. These included the fostering of closer technical co-operation within the Group and the temporary pooling of resources between UK companies in order to finance global projects. An example of the former was the collaboration between JBE and Vosper of Barrow to design and manufacture an escape gangway for use in North Sea oil platform evacuations. The latter was demonstrated by the formation in September 1984 of United Offshore Limited. This consortium, comprising JBE and Constructors International Limited, in collaboration with Matthew Hall International Limited and Cleveland Redpath Offshore Limited (a Trafalgar House subsidiary company), was established specifically to win design and construction work for the emerging Chinese offshore oil and gas industry.

The Men and the Management
On the industrial relations front, Raymond McCabe continued the process first begun in 1980 by Graham Strachan: to tackle the inherited legacy of unproductive working practices and the many demarcation disputes. The resolution of these particular problems has been largely attributed to Personnel Director, Dick Cummings, who had joined the company in July 1980 from British Leyland. Starting with a Product Cost Review and new productivity programmes, Dick Cummings initiated a series of personnel changes that (almost uniquely in this field) kept JBE free from strikes and disputes from 1982 until 1999! Almost from the day he was appointed, Dick Cummings was forced, as he saw it, "to take on the Unions"[i]. With approximately thirteen different Unions involved, his first challenge was to resolve the tendency of the numerous bargaining groups to play "leap frog"[ii] with one another during the annual wage

Dick Cummings, JBE Personnel Director (third from left) with Gordon Maclennan, Gavin Laird (President of the AEEU) and Raymond McCabe

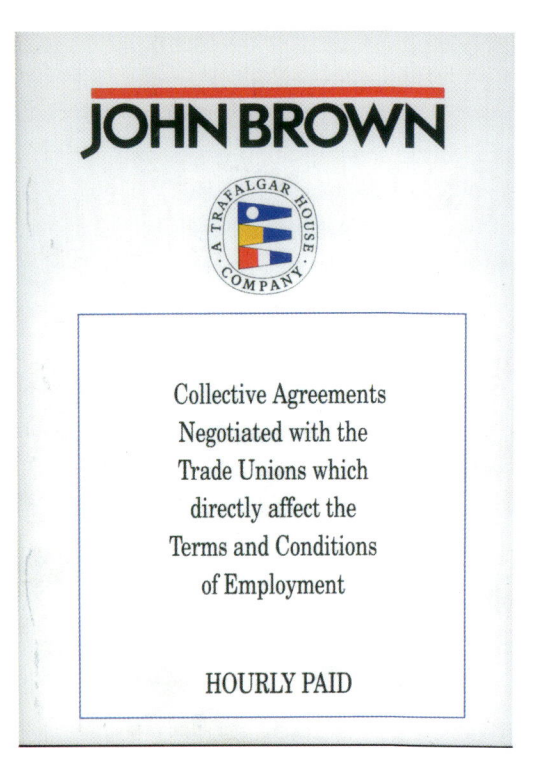

Collective Agreements booklet

negotiations. In effect, whenever one set of workers achieved a wage increase, or a concession over working practices, this would immediately result in a clamour from the other Unions for parity. When he stopped this practice, the company was initially threatened with strike action. However, his determination, allied with fairness and even-handedness, led to the workforce in time becoming more receptive. Undoubtedly, however, Dick Cummings' major breakthrough was the introduction of a substantive Flexibility Agreement on 30 June 1982.[iii] This was a collective agreement negotiated with the various Unions affecting the terms and conditions of employment of all hourly-paid workers, whereby the company agreed to honour the current national agreements, but would not be bound by future national agreements after 30 June 1982. This Agreement was a watershed in working practices within the industry and was, reputedly, not only the first cross-Union flexibility deal on Clydeside, but one of the first in the UK.

In late 1981 Dick Cummings had also introduced job evaluation, and a number of equal opportunities and health and safety policies. Although no concessions were offered to the workforce, the job evaluation exercise (which reduced the numbers of grades) did result in better wage levels for most workers. More importantly, however, was the management's decision to move away from the traditional management-Union relationship, and the elitist 'them and us' attitude, and instead view the entire workforce (including management) simply as employees. The new style of management was put across by Raymond McCabe when he initiated a series of video presentations to the workforce in 1984. This refreshingly modern approach manifested itself in many ways, not least the canteen facilities! Whereas previously there had been separate canteens for senior management, staff and workers, under Raymond McCabe there was one facility shared by all personnel.

Attempts to strengthen JBE

The continuing financial problems of the parent company (and JBE), however, left Raymond McCabe little room for manoeuvre. Despite posting modest profits in the two years up to 1984, JBE, like the parent company, was not expected to return to profit until 1985-86. Further, JBE was burdened with high financing costs of £30m per annum, making it an ideal candidate for disposal by the parent company. The continuing uncertainty created by the almost constant speculation about likely buyers, was further heightened by the uncertainty of the power engineering business. With demand for gas turbines and accessories fluctuating widely from year to year, companies such as JBE found it extremely difficult to plan ahead to ensure a reasonable return on their operations, and constant employment for their workforce. JBE's difficulties were also compounded by their reliance on a single product, i.e., gas turbines, and the fact that they were heavily dependent on the goodwill of GE.

In recognising this vulnerability, Raymond McCabe initiated, and led, a major review of JBE's strategic direction. In the main, the conclusions of the review were:
- JBE would need to continue as a manufacturer of GE gas turbines.
- With many opportunities for selling JBE manufactured gas turbines being lost due to the company's lack of total contract capability, the Operations Division would be expanded to become a "Total Power Plant Contractor".
- Due to fluctuations in demand for Gas Turbines, the Manufacturing Division would diversify into other products.
- Customer Services Division would be strengthened at the top and expanded to provide a complete range of after sales services, thus becoming the anchor of the JBE business.
- New markets with new products would be urgently sought.

These conclusions were implemented with all speed and were to have a significant impact on the future of the company, steering it out of the doldrums through what were the best ten years of JBE's life.

The main thrust of the review had been announced to the workforce in early 1984, when Raymond McCabe made a second video presentation to all employees. He stressed that potential clients had to be convinced that JBE was no longer exclusively a gas turbine company. As he put it, "we are called John Brown Engineering, not John Brown Gas Turbines"![iv]

In order to achieve the goals of the new strategic direction, it was also necessary for Raymond McCabe to build his own management team. The development of the Operations Division into a total power plant contractor was entrusted to the then Projects Director, Alan Young, who was appointed Operations Director in 1984. Norman Simpson had already taken over as Finance Director when Raymond McCabe became Managing Director. Gordon Maclennan was recruited to strengthen the Manufacturing team and was soon to become Manufacturing Director on the resignation of Harry Crawford. Alan Young's depute, Jack Bell, was set the task of finding new markets with new products that could fit into JBE's capability and skills.

One of the changes initiated by Jack Bell was the formation of a Manufacturing Development Department, whose principal function was to utilise Engine and Fabrication Works capacity to help support the gas turbine programme, and to develop the capability to manufacture related products (including non-gas turbine work for oil-related petro-chemical industries and the Ministry of Defence).

An artist's reproduction of an escape gangway for use on the North Sea oil platform supply ship, Iolair

A ten strong sales team under Manager Jim Barr was set up and, within a year of commencing operation, Jim was able to announce that various projects equivalent to 40,000 man hours had been completed. These included the manufacture of leg tensioning equipment for stabilising offshore platform legs, launching skids to enable remote control vehicles to be positioned on the sea bed, escape gangways for oil platform supply ships, mill housings and coal storage silos for the cement industry, and the refurbishing of water turbine main inlet valves.

Video presentation by Raymond McCabe in the Works canteen, 1984

By the end of 1984 the company had manufactured over 400 gas turbines for operation in forty-three countries throughout the world since the signing of the original MA Agreement in 1965. Significantly, 38 per cent of these turbines had been supplied to five clients. In the case of two - the Russian and Algerian purchasing agencies (Machinoimport and Sonatrach) - these turbines were mechanical drive units driving compressors for pipelines (the former contract alone accounting for 17 per cent of JBE's total output). In respect of the other three - Abu Dhabi Water & Electricity Department, British Petroleum and the British Smelter Construction - the turbines supplied were for power generation. Importantly, whereas the early contracts were largely quite simple, involving the manufacture of standard Frame 3 and 5 gas turbines, which could be completed within an average of six months, the later contracts were more complex. These involved Frame 6, 7 and 9s which, on average, took up to three years to complete, from the placing of the original order to commissioning of the completed power plant. The gas turbine world market at this time was dominated by GE and its MAs who accounted for 58 per cent of the market. The remaining 42 per cent was shared by Brown Boveri, Siemens, GEC, Rolls Royce, and Westinghouse and its licensees.

However, despite the various measures taken by JBE, and the winning of orders worth over £28m for new gas turbines, the company was still struggling. In September 1984 parts of JBE's Works temporarily initiated a four-day working week. Scheduled to last until 29 December, this was caused by a slump in demand for engineering goods. While job losses were avoided by this measure, it was calculated that the hourly-paid workers lost approximately half-a-day's wages each week.

Water and Sewerage: a new opportunity

Of the many different markets explored by Jack Bell and his team, the one that was to play a significant part in the future of the company was water and sewerage. This was initiated in response to the privatisation of the industry by Margaret Thatcher's Conservative government in 1988. Together with new EEC legislation designed to improve the standard of drinking water, this provided companies such as JBE with an opportunity to generate new business as the newly privatised companies undertook a massive investment programme in new plant. Although initially the new Division struggled to secure suitable contracts, by the late 1980s the company felt sufficiently confident to strengthen the now named Process Services Division and appoint Tom Gray as its General Manager.

Ultimately, the scale and complexity of these modernisation schemes meant that even the largest firms found it necessary to pool resources within their group, or enter into partnership with competitors. Likewise, the private utilities involved were compelled to enter into joint ventures to fund the schemes. Sometimes these ventures would be in the form of Build-Own-Operate (BOO) agreements - an early form of Private Finance Initiative (PFI). In the early 1990s, in order to win some of this business, JBE combined with, for example, sister company, Cementation Construction. They also worked in partnership with Thistle House (Major Projects), a consortium specially formed by Trafalgar House to undertake this type of work. This partnership was reasonably successful, being awarded several major contracts by companies, such as South West Water and Severn Trent Water.

By 1991 the Process Services Division employed almost two hundred personnel and was considered to be among the top ten companies operating in this specialised field. At that time the Division had over £80m worth of contracts, including Frankley and Strensham in England, and Alloa in Scotland. The Frankley and Strensham contracts (both undertaken for Severn Trent Water) were notable for using leading edge technology. At the Frankley Water Treatment Works near Birmingham, for example, the £50m modernisation works utilised the latest Dissolved Air Flotation (DAF) process to purify and improve the taste of the treated water. After completion of the refurbishment, Frankley was capable of supplying 450m litres of water (as opposed to 320m litres previously) to homes and businesses around Birmingham. At Strensham, an alternative process known as Granular Activated Carbon (GAC), was installed.

Another water and sewerage project was the upgrading of a 1950's built water treatment plant at Ogston in Derbyshire, to meet the new EC regulations. This £900,000 contract, awarded by Severn Trent Water, was for the design, supply and installation of sterilisation and related systems. In 1990 JBE won a £1.63m contract for the refurbishment and extension of Central Regional Council's Alloa Sewage Treatment Works. As main mechanical and electrical contractor, JBE undertook (in conjunction with the engineering consultants) all design, supply and commissioning work, to ensure that the effluent discharged into the River Forth would meet EC effluent standards.

A contract from Thames Water Utilities Limited was won in 1990. This was worth £1.7m, and was for the extension and modification of their Newbury Sewage Treatment Works near Reading. Also included in the contract was the supply of a computerised monitoring system.

These contracts were different from the gas turbine power station contracts, in that there was greater integration with civil engineering works where Trafalgar House Companies had particular and well-established strengths. It was determined at Group level that JBE should withdraw from this activity and consequently in 1993 several major contracts were handed over by JBE to other Group Companies. Thereafter JBE concentrated exclusively on Power Generation activities.

---

i Interview with Dick Cummings on 12 November, 2001.
ii Interview with Dick Cummings on 12 November, 2001.
iii *Collective Agreements Negotiated with the Trade Unions which directly affect the Terms and Conditions of Employment*, (n.d.), (booklet).
iv *JB News* (1984), April/May.

9   JBE in Trafalgar House

Trafalgar House steps in

By the mid-1980s the performance of the parent company, now only "a shadow of its former self",[i] continued to concern its shareholders. At that time it was believed that the parent company's only hope was to reduce costs and further expand its product range, while awaiting an upturn in the market. The troubled power engineering division was of particular concern. Closure of JBE was not viable because of the cost implications, and since there was still no prospect of a 'white knight' coming forward, the parent company had little option but to ride out the storm. The prospects for 1986 for the parent company seemed more promising: John Cuckney's earlier disposals programme had reduced the 1984 pre-tax loss of £5.6m by £1.1m in the financial year ending 31 March 1985.

Despite the parent company's continued optimism that they could ultimately resolve their financial difficulties, they were obliged in June 1985 to apply for a temporary suspension of their shares (then valued at 33p) to allow a recovery programme to be agreed with their bankers. The principal objective of these negotiations was to substantially reduce the parent company's debts of over £120m by converting some of the debt into equity, and issuing new shares. The subsequent re-capitalisation proposals agreed with the banks were accepted by shareholders in August 1985. These also included acceptance of an offer by the giant UK construction conglomerate, Trafalgar House plc, to take a 29.9 per cent minority financial stake in the re-vitalised company - a move regarded by most City analysts as being a prelude to an eventual full take-over. Their new business partner had been founded in 1956 by Sir Nigel Broackes. Trafalgar House had expanded into the construction and engineering field in 1984 by acquiring Scott Lithgow (the loss-making shipbuilding yard) and RGC Offshore, as well as embarking in a joint venture with the Davy Corporation, to form Trafalgar Davy Offshore. The re-constituted Board of John Brown & Company Limited (strengthened by the addition of three Trafalgar House Directors) forecast a loss of £3.3m in 1985: a slight improvement on the £4.5m loss forecast in 1984.

Ominously for Clydebank, however, gas turbine sales had plummeted from over £56m to just over £8m, due in part to worse than expected trading conditions and the high cost of sterling. The latter particularly affected export trade, and consequently JBE, which relied largely on exporting. Although strenuous efforts were made by the Clydebank management to improve profit margins by, for example, reducing stock levels and operating costs, the worsening conditions meant JBE had to implement further redundancies.

Within Trafalgar House itself, the Board's venture into John Brown & Company Limited was not universally well-received by shareholders, who (still smarting over the poor short term returns from the Scott Lithgow and Davy acquisitions) began to ask questions of the Board. The Board, however, argued that the minority stake in John Brown & Company Limited was a longer-term investment which would allow Trafalgar House to better compete in the international oil and gas market. And, notwithstanding these shareholder concerns, in May 1986, Trafalgar House's Chief Executive Eric Parker announced his intention to bid £80m for the still financially troubled John Brown & Company Limited. Being already in the shipping, construction and property markets, this acquisition would increase the Trafalgar House portfolio. In particular, it was believed that the addition of the Group's process engineering expertise, especially in the manufacture of heavy duty industrial gas turbines, would enable Trafalgar House to pursue major turnkey engineering and construction contracts both in the UK and overseas. Allan Gormly saw the advantages that the greater resources of the combined companies would bring to John Brown & Company Limited, for instance in bidding for major turnkey contracts, and, since he found the offer acceptable, endorsed the Trafalgar House bid. Accordingly, in mid-1986, John Brown & Company Limited (and with it, JBE) became part of Trafalgar House plc. This latest acquisition continued to concern Trafalgar House shareholders, despite a 26 per cent increase in pre-tax profits to approximately £72m. With John Brown & Company anticipating a pre-tax loss, and the failure of the Trafalgar-Davy consortium to secure North Sea contracts, they considered it highly unlikely that there would be any short-term return on their investment.

In 1986 there was a brief, but welcome, respite from the constant struggle to find new work when JBE participated in Clydebank District Council's Centenary Year celebrations. Throughout that year JBE

Operations Director, Alaister Forsyth

HRH Queen Elizabeth in discussion with JBE employee, Charles Shields, during her tour of Engine Works, August 1986. Also present are Customer Services Division General Manager, Mike Pell, and Managing Director, Raymond McCabe

Family and friends at the Works, August 1986

supported many of the events. They also sponsored the cultivation of a unique Centenary Rose, the resulting profits from sales going to help St. Margaret's Hospice, Clydebank. The celebrations culminated in the visit of HRH Queen Elizabeth II who sailed up the River Clyde on 9 August 1986 in the John Brown built Royal Yacht *Britannia*. Landing at Rothesay Dock, the Queen toured JBE. To mark the occasion, a Family Day was arranged for the workforce, and the Works were thrown open to family and friends.

The Projects

During the second half of the 1980s, despite the continuing market fluctuations, JBE were successful in securing a number of highly significant orders from, among others, China, the Philippines and the UK.

Of particular note were a series of further Chinese contracts for single and combined cycle plants worth £88m. These were placed by the Huaneng International Power Development Corporation (HIPDC) which had been established in the early 1980s by the Chinese Prime Minister to oversee a massive modernisation of the Chinese electricity supply industry. The first of these contracts, ultimately worth £47m, was for combined cycle power stations at Liao He, Shengli and Zhong Yuan. This contract had

HRH Queen Elizabeth (with Clydebank Provost, David Grainger) carrying a basket of the JBE-sponsored Clydebank Centenary Rose Photograph reproduced courtesy of Holmes of Clydebank

effectively been snatched from under the noses of French rivals, Alsthom. In the July of that year, a price had been agreed by the Chinese with Alsthom for two of the three power stations, leaving JBE to compete only for the third and last station. However, noting that the French bid was being backed by financial assistance from the French government, JBE lobbied the UK government for similar assistance, and was ultimately able to offer an Aid and Trade Provision (ATP) package worth almost £5m. Initially, the ATP package only applied to the Shengli Power Station, but, following further lobbying by JBE it was extended to cover all three stations, and the Chinese were persuaded to accept all three projects as one contract. A later analysis conducted by the University of Strathclyde's Fraser of Allander Institute found that the ATP package for these three contracts had, among other benefits, created 1,757 additional man-years of work, and that in total some 1,050 UK companies had gained from the contract. [ii]

JBE's success in gaining this contract also led to the placing of further Chinese power station contracts worth an additional £35m. The first of these was placed in 1987 by the China National Machinery Import & Export Corporation (CNM) for a simple cycle power station on Hainan Island, Southern China. This was the fastest ever contract fulfilled by JBE: in less than three months from the signing of the contract the two Frame 5 gas turbines were ready for shipping out and site construction commenced on 24 January 1988. By April of that year, both turbines had been commissioned and accepted by CNM, and two days later the Power Station was officially opened. In 1988 three further contracts were placed by HIPDC, the Liuzhou Zhen-Xing Power Company, and the Nanning City Gas Turbine Power Generating Company. The first of these contracts was for a combined cycle power station at Chongqing in Sichuan province and the second (worth approximately £4m) was for the supply of a power station at Liuzhou. The last was a simple cycle power station north of Hainan Island.

The Chongqing project was a particularly challenging one, as all the equipment and plant required for the power station had to be transported on barges thousands of miles up the Yangzte River, through the many spectacular river gorges, to reach Chongqing. Typically, this journey took an average of two to three weeks. Built to supplement the power from nearby hydro-electric schemes, the station was powered by two Frame 6 gas turbines, running on natural gas piped in from the nearby gas fields. In addition to supplying the gas turbines, JBE also had responsibility for all site works (including a highly computerised central control room), and the training of local personnel to operate the finished power station. During the contract, close links were developed with the Mayor of Chongqing, Sun Tongchuan, who, as well as being a frequent visitor to the site, made regular visits to Clydebank while work was in progress.

As with earlier Chinese contracts won during the 1970s, this latest series of contracts were secured after many months of lengthy and complex negotiation by the sales team - on this occasion led by Sales Director, Bob Hepburn. During these negotiations, the sales team would sometimes be required to work seven days a week, dealing with anything from six to forty Chinese officials. Contract conditions, while demanding, were fair. However, whilst highly profitable, the contracts in many ways posed numerous logistical problems. Typically, up until the last minute, the sales team would be unaware of both the location of the sites and the number of units required. The clients would demand that, regardless of any design changes, the original costs should be adhered to (although payment was always timeous) and that Chinese civil and engineering sub-contractors should be used. The unreliability of these sub-contractors created extreme difficulties, leading to delays. There were also problems with travel arrangements and site accommodation for JBE personnel. On one occasion, although site works had been completed on time, the power station was unable to function for a considerable period because there was no gas to power it!

In 1988 JBE won another challenging and innovative contract, on this occasion for five 38mw power generation barges and five fuel-carrying barges. These were floating power plants which could be moved to wherever there was the greatest need for power. This contract, placed by the National Power Corporation of the Philippines, was worth £41m and led Raymond McCabe to declare that "our name is now as internationally famous as it was when we launched the *Queen Elizabeth* fifty years ago and later the *QE2*".[iii] Following confirmation

One of the six power generation barges under construction in the PNOC Dockyard, Philippines

of this contract, messages of congratulation were received from the then Scottish Secretary of State, Malcolm Rifkind, and the STUC General Secretary, Campbell Christie, the latter declaring that "world class"[iv] JBE had been successful because, among other things, they had "excellent worker-management relations".[v] As usual, the order was secured in the face of fierce competition, and was won thanks to the ingenuity of JBE's design team who devised a scheme to construct six floating platforms, which could "plug in to the nearest power station".[vi] Whereas the gas turbines and associated equipment were built in Clydebank and shipped to the Philippines, the barges were constructed in the PNOC Dockyard & Engineering Corporation yard at Batangas Bay (300 miles south of Manila Bay).

One of the main features of the 1980s was an increasing focus on environmental issues. These had first surfaced in the mid-1970s, amid concerns about the possible harmful effects of global warming from so called 'holes' in the ozone layer caused by the use of chlorofluorocarbons

Peterhead Power Station - the UK's first 'clean' power station

(CFCs), etc. Specific concerns in the early 1980s about the harmful effects of power station emissions, brought with it a potentially lucrative opportunity for companies engaged in the power generation industry. Up until that point, the US and Eastern Europe in particular had not accepted that emissions of, for example, sulphur and nitrogen oxides, could cause widespread environmental damage, commonly referred to as 'acid rain'. In June 1983, however, with forests and lakes in Canada and the North Eastern United States badly affected by chemical blight, the American government decided to reduce these emissions, and their lead was followed by European governments. This led to a demand for the installation of desulphurisation equipment in the UK's older coal-fired power stations. Although JBE responded to these environmental concerns by taking out a GEESI licence with GE in 1986, its failure to secure significant contracts (such as the Drax Power Station conversion) led to this work being given over to the larger Engineering & Construction

One of the massive Frame 9 gas turbines en route to Peterhead

Division in London, who thereafter handled all such projects.

Another significant contract won in the late 1980s, in the face of intense competition from Europe and America was the £40m turnkey contract for Scottish Hydro-Electric's Peterhead Power Station. This was a ground-breaking contract as, not only was it Britain's first 'clean' power station, but the first major power station to be built in Britain using gas turbines powered by North Sea natural gas. Built as a back-up for the existing power station at Peterhead, it was based on two JBE-built Frame 9E gas turbines. These turbines (then the largest of their type in the world) each weighed 277 tons and (in their containers) measured 30 metres long by 6 metres high. The first of the turbines was shipped out of Rothesay Dock in early 1991, with the second leaving the following month.

By 1989, Trafalgar House was in a much stronger position. In the financial year ending

September, record breaking results were reported, with turnover up by 21 per cent and profits by 18 per cent. This vastly improved performance was reflected in more favourable media coverage for the Group. However, following a sharp increase in oil prices caused by the Iraq-Iran war, the second half of the following year saw the situation deteriorate, so that in the financial year ending September 1990 profits were down from £270.4m to £155.7m. Notwithstanding, turnover and profits within the Engineering & Construction arm (and, by implication, JBE) were up by 18 and 19 per cent respectively.

This better than expected performance, and the likelihood of new orders, left JBE confident to expand and diversify. Consequently, a Panels & Systems unit was established within the Manufacturing Division to manufacture a range of computerised control panels for power projects. In 1990, on the strength of having won more than a quarter of a billion pounds worth of orders for projects in Australia, China, Hong Kong, Morocco, the USA and

The Penny's Bay Power Station, Hong Kong, which JBE completed in under two years

the Middle East, JBE were awarded their fifth Queen's Award for Export Achievement. At this time JBE had exported 454 gas turbines to fifty different countries!

Also in that year, JBE secured a major contract (a joint venture between themselves, China Light & Power Company and Exxon) for a 300mw Power Station at Penny's Bay, Lantau Island in Hong Kong's New Territories. This power station was designed to operate as a stand-by facility in the event of there being a failure in the existing power station, and also to provide spare capacity for the anticipated future power requirements of the area. Therefore, the power station (which had an operational life expectancy of twenty-five years) was suitable for both normal and off-peak electricity demands. As well as the construction of a turbine hall and the supply of three Frame 9E gas turbines, the contract also included all design work and shipping.

Channel Island Power Station, Darwin, Australia

In late 1990, having previously supplied sixteen gas turbines to Australian clients (including what was Australia's first combined cycle gas turbine plant at the Channel Island Power Station, Darwin), JBE announced the award of two further contracts worth a total of £22.5m. The first of these contracts was placed by the State Energy Commission of Western Australia (SECWA) for a 105mw power station being constructed as part of the Pinjar project, designed for both off peak and base load operations, to supplement the outputs from Muja, Kwinana and Bunbury Power Stations. Included in the contract was the supply of two Frame 9 gas turbines built to run on either natural gas or oil distillate, and designed to convert to combined cycle if later required. The second contract was for a 35mw

The signing of Serdang/Pasir Gudang contract in Kuala Lumpur. Those present include: Raymond McCabe; UK Prime Minister John Major; the Prime Minister of Malaysia, Y Bhg Dato Seri Dr. Mahathir Bin Mohamad; and Dr. Ani Bin Arope, Executive Chairman TNB

power station for Mount Isa Mines Limited for their Mica Creek site in Queensland. The Mount Isa mine was then one of the world's leading producers of copper and silver-lead-zinc, producing five million tons each of copper and silver-lead-zinc ore each year. As part of the contract, JBE supplied one Frame 6 turbine (with an option for a second turbine), to provide additional power for the facility.

Unfortunately, Christmas Day 1992 brought some distressing news for JBE. Mike Pell was informed of a serious incident at a power station in Newark, New Jersey, operated and

A Frame 9E gas turbine being loaded onto a freighter for transporting to Malaysia, 1993

maintained by JBE. Mike Pell and Chris Packard immediately went to Newark to investigate. A leak within a flexible coupling in the steam turbine lubrication system had sprayed lubricating oil onto a heater, causing a serious fire. Sadly, it resulted in the deaths of three US employees.

Between 1993 and 1994, Tenaga Nasional Berhad (TNB) ordered a further five Frame 9s for sites in Malaysia. These two contracts were part of an Accelerated Power Development

HRH Prince Charles with JBE officials, John Glover and Stephen Griffin, at a Trade Fair in Casablanca, 1995

Project to meet the rapidly growing demand for electricity in the country. The units were designed to run on either natural gas or distillate oil, so that in the event of a power disruption they could switch to a standby oil supply, stored in two 12,000 ton tanks, providing sufficient fuel for twenty days. One of the contracts was a turnkey project at Serdang worth £120m. This plant comprised two simple cycle Frame 9E gas turbines which, with a mind to future expansion, could be converted to combined cycle. Uniquely, because of lack of water, the aluminium clad turbine hall required to be supplied with a cooling system which drew moisture from the air. The other contract was for a 330mw power station at Pasir Gudang, equipped with three simple cycle Frame 9E gas turbines.

The TNB contracts were followed by an announcement in November 1993 that JBE had secured a contract to extend and modify a power generating and distillation plant at Al Ghubrah in Oman. This turnkey contract, awarded by the Ministry of Electricity and Water in Oman, was for the construction of a 250mw co-generation plant designed to convert the waste heat from the two Frame 9E gas turbines into steam for a new desalination plant, thereby increasing efficiency by 82 per cent.

A further major order followed in December 1994, when JBE secured a contract to supply a 300mw combined cycle power station for the Zhejiang Zhenhai United Power Company Limited in Ningbo City, Zhenhai province in China.

In addition to the contracts for Frame 9 turbines, the company also procured a number of orders for Frame 6 units in the early 1990s. This included a £100m order from WED for twelve Frame 6 heavy duty gas turbines for two Abu Dhabi installations, and a £32m contract for three Frame 6 gas turbines for the first power station to be built in Morocco by a UK company.

Structural Changes

A much welcomed improvement in the fortunes of Trafalgar House at the end of the 1980s had continued into the next decade with a pre-tax profit of £122.4m. Despite the continuing recession affecting the UK and US markets, Sir Nigel Broackes felt that significant progress had been made in re-shaping the Group for the future. Aside from reducing costs and implementing redundancies, the rights issue in July 1991 had raised £312m. Furthermore, parts of the cargo shipping business had been sold to P&O for £41m, and debts totalling £20m had been transferred from the Group. In addition, Davy Corporation plc had been acquired. This was seen as a particularly significant move for, like John Brown & Company Limited, Davy was involved in metal processing, and oil, gas and petrochemicals, on an international scale. The merging of these two interests, in effect, created one of the largest such groups in the world.

Of all the Divisions, Engineering & Construction had perhaps fared better in the climate of poor trading conditions, posting a record operating profit of £82.3m, and with an order book at an all time high of £3bn. A similar picture was reported within the Division's Power Engineering and Water & Sewage Treatment sectors, where demand had remained steady.

In late 1992, despite annual sales in excess of £4bn, Trafalgar House was still struggling financially. These difficulties resulted in major boardroom changes that saw Alan Clements appointed Group Chairman in place of Sir Nigel Broakes, and Allan Gormly promoted to the position of Group Chief Executive. A further significant development (trumpeted as the beginning of a "new era for Trafalgar House"[vii]) was the appearance of a major investor: in October 1992 a Hong Kong based property company, Hongkong Land Holdings Limited initiated a dawn raid to acquire a 14.9 per cent stake in Trafalgar House.

(Left to right) Allan Gormly, Sir John Cuckney, Mikhail Gorbachev, and interpreter Richard Pollock, at John Brown Headquarters in London, 1985

Although an immediate attempt to raise their holding to 29.9 per cent was defeated, in February 1993 Hongkong Land did succeed in further increasing their stake to 20.1 per cent. As part of the Jardine Matheson Group, Hongkong Land were already linked to Trafalgar House through the jointly-owned construction company, Gammon Construction Limited (Hong Kong). By increasing their holding, it was felt Hongkong Land had signalled their intention to play a more significant role in the future of Trafalgar House. This move was welcomed by Allan Gormly, who viewed the Hongkong Land investment as a long-term initiative, and one which would help the future expansion and development of Trafalgar House.

Despite a pre-tax loss of £30.3m in 1992, Allan Gormly still regarded Trafalgar House as a major international player, and one of Britain's leading exporters. Bolstered by their new investor, the Group initiated the disposal of further non-core business and property, and re-structured their passenger fleet, Cunard. This latest rationalisation was intended to allow the slimmed down Group to concentrate on engineering and construction which, it was felt, could be more profitable.

However, as 1993 wore on, the position within Trafalgar House worsened, leading to the appointment of their third Chairman in the space of two years when Jardine Matheson's

Simon Keswick replaced Alan Clements. At the same time Nigel Rich (Jardine Matheson's Managing Director) replaced Allan Gormly as Chief Executive Officer.

In October, to avoid unhelpful market speculation, the financially crippled Group presented its full year results early. In an attempt to avoid the need for any ill-judged "fire sale disposals",[viii] for the third time in about two years the Group sought to raise additional cash from its shareholders. The £400m raised on this occasion meant that, since 1987 (when the first rights issue had taken place) the Group had raised approximately £1,230m through the use of this device. In December, Nigel Rich re-iterated the need to sell off more properties, including the prestigious Ritz Hotel in London. The cash raised from this latest rights issue was largely channelled into the Engineering & Construction Division which, with an annual turnover of around £3,500m, required access to substantial guaranteed cash credits in order to fulfil the bonding requirements placed on major contracts.

The presentation of JBE's sixth Queens Award to Raymond McCabe by Lord Lieutenant Brigadier Donald Hardie, 1994

Whereas Trafalgar House's trading position had worsened during the early 1990s, JBE's four Clydebank Divisions had, by contrast, enjoyed a period of enormous growth and profitability. During this period JBE, in addition to receiving public recognition from Glasgow District Council, won two further Queen's Awards for Export Achievement and were twice GE's biggest customer. Perhaps most fittingly, their outstanding performance led to the award of a CBE to Managing Director, Raymond McCabe.

Their success was also demonstrated by a dramatic increase in personnel. By 1994, in contrast to the 800 employed in the mid-1980s, JBE had 1,800 personnel, of whom 1,200 were permanent. These permanent employees represented a mix of skills that the management believed it required to give the company a sustainable long-term future, whilst the temporary employees were needed to meet the surge in demand from across the world.

Finding sufficient qualified and experienced engineers in the UK had not been easy, and the company was forced to recruit from overseas, notably India and Hong Kong. Staff shortages were to play a significant part in the ultimate demise of the business, as JBE was unable to start, and hence finish, its contracts on time.

Although problems with the major turnkey contracts in both Power and Water & Sewerage were building up by 1994, both Manufacturing and Customer Services Divisions were contributing significantly to the company's growth and profit. Output from manufacturing, although bolstered by the major contracts within the Operations Division, reached half-a-million man hours in a year, and for the first time in many years not only covered its full overhead cost, but also contributed to the company's profits. Despite this apparent success within the Manufacturing Division, management still did not believe that there was a long term future for the Division meriting the level of investment required if it was to become competitive worldwide. Whilst the existence of the factory and the manufacture of gas turbines at Clydebank was still considered essential to the future of the company, management believed that there were other much more pressing priorities for capital investment.

As the Operations Division expanded, so it had to modernise. This, however, would require very considerable investment. Initially there was great reluctance by the staff to move from the draughtsman's pencil and the tracer's pen to the computer. Frustrated by the reluctance for change, and to force home the modernisation of the Division, Raymond McCabe ordered the scrapping of all drawing boards, and a new age dawned. As the Division continued to expand with the remarkable success of the Sales Department in securing more orders, investment was not only in computers and training, but also in bricks and mortar. Offices at Whitecrook and Manchester were opened. On the surface JBE was very successful, with turnover approaching £400m and acceptable profits being made. By the mid-90s, however, dark clouds were starting to gather. As problems began to multiply, questions were asked. Had the company been over ambitious and taken on too much work? Was the Operations Division capable of managing these mega projects? By 1995 the problems were amassing at such a rate that it was beginning to look as though they would wipe out all the not inconsiderable profits made during the first half of the decade.

As the Operations Division on the Power side was having its problems, problems were also developing on the Water & Sewerage side. The characteristics of the Power and Water & Sewerage businesses were quite different, with the behaviour of the latter more akin to that of the construction industry. It was perhaps the lack of appreciation of this at both local and main Board levels that forced JBE to exit this market in mid-1995. Also, Trafalgar House's encouragement to its companies to expand into new markets did nothing to control the competition that was developing between Group companies. This was not only in relation to those competing with each other, but also between those who were supposedly working together in consortium or other similar commercial arrangement. Some believed that this side of the business was aborted before it was given adequate time to prove itself: whilst the loss making water contracts had a huge constraining effect on cash flow, many years later when all debts had been received and the cost of interest ignored, these contracts broke even.

Part of Raymond McCabe's strategy had been to build as many arms of the JBE businesses as possible so that, when part of the business was suffering hardship, the other parts would be there to support. In the mid-1980s, when setting out his strategy, he had seen a pivotal role for the after sales service of gas turbines. In particular he recognised that whilst parts of the business may well fluctuate substantially, customer service should be built into a business with a regular profit contribution. Following his appointment in 1986, Chris Packard set out his vision for the CSD and within a few years had moved the Division from a spares and services organisation to an enterprise that was able to offer professional and immediate after sales service to its customers. At its cornerstone were long term operation and maintenance contracts which provided steady work, thus evening out the ups and downs of the overall business. Privatisation in the UK had brought a completely new demand for after sales service similar to that in the USA, where the company had already been operating for a number of years. In the States it was normal for owners to reduce their financial exposure by sub-contracting the entire operation and maintenance of their power plants, indeed the banks even demanded that they do so. Despite the tragedy which befell one of the Newark plants operated by the company, invaluable experience was gained in the management and handling of long term operation and maintenance contracts in the USA, equipping the CSD team well able to deal with the new scene in the UK.

Throughout the 1990s, CSD provided profits of more than £5m each year. To some extent the Division's profits were enhanced by the success of the main Sales team in the early days. It was, however, the modernisation of the Division in 1993/94 that proved to be the real turning point. Not satisfied that the focus of the Division was right, or that the quality of service was adequate, Chris Packard decided to find out what the customers expected, and wanted. Teams were sent out across the world and customer surveys carried out, not by management, but by staff within the Division, and the results analysed. These proved to be a revelation. One customer had no less than twenty-three separate points of contact for the various services he required. The surveys were a great success, since everyone became aware of the work that needed to be done to achieve the vision for the Division "as the best customer service team in the world". It took a year to change all the existing practices, and train and introduce customer-focused teams as a single point of contact, with teams of specialists supporting them. The most novel feature was that it was up to the support teams to sell their services competitively to the customer teams, who were free to obtain support services from wherever they wished. This was a great success with the customers, although some members of staff were never comfortable with the concept of having 'internal' customers!

Despite attempts by GE to buy this highly successful business, CSD (together with Masaoood John Brown, its successful joint venture company in the Middle East), remained as a vital part of the Clydebank business. It never adopted a high profile stance, but became the anchor that provided the lifeline to both JBE and KEL through its last years under Kvaerner.

Keadby

Of the several major contracts secured in the early 1990s, undoubtedly the most significant was a £267m contract for a 677mw combined cycle gas turbine power station at Keadby, near Scunthorpe, South Humberside, on the site of a former Central Electricity Generating Board (CEGB) coal fired power station. This contract - for the world's first 9F combined cycle power plant - was signed in April 1992. Although rightly heralded at the time as a

Keadby Power Station under construction

major coup for the company, it ultimately proved to be one of the most disastrous in the company's history, and cost JBE over £30m in penalties.

The aim of the project, which had become possible with the privatisation of the UK electricity supply industry, was to produce electricity for sale to the National Grid. It had been initiated by Scottish Hydro-Electric but, realising it was too big for them to handle on their own, they formed a partnership with North West Electricity Board (NORWEB) to create an Independent Power Producer (IPP) trading as Keadby Power Limited (KPL). Since the viability of the project very much depended on the production costs of the electricity generated, serious consideration was given to the model of gas turbine to be used. It was soon realised that the only suitable model was GE's new, and relatively unproven, Frame 9F gas turbine. In light of the later difficulties, the reliability of this model became a matter of fierce debate. As was usual with such contracts, there was provision for compensation in the

A Frame 9F gas turbine en route to Keadby

A Frame 9F gas turbine being manoeuvered into position in the Turbine Hall, Keadby

event that the technology proved unequal to its task, but the maximum liquidated damages claimable against GE was not back-to-back with JBE. As turnkey operator, JBE had responsibility for the project management, design, engineering, procurement, construction, testing and commissioning. However, unusually for JBE, nearly all of the turbines and accessories were sub-contracted out. Thus, the two Frame 9F gas turbines came from GE; the generators and steam turbine generator from GEC/Alsthom; and two waste heat recovery boilers from Babcock Energy. In addition to the construction of a gas turbine hall, steam turbine hall, administration and control room building and pumphouse, JBE was required to oversee the construction of a cooling water system (taking water from, and returning it to, the nearby River Trent), a water treatment plant and liquid fuel storage facilities.

The team assembled by JBE to project manage this work was headed by Bill Law, who reported to Geoff Mexon (General Manager - Projects) and, ultimately, Operations Director, Willie Forrest. Initially work progressed according to plan towards the anticipated completion date of January 1995. Raymond McCabe, who viewed this contract as a watershed in JBE's history, later recalled that while all works were completed close to schedule, the gas turbines failed at the commissioning stage. During the initial running of the turbines, damage was caused to the rotor blades by high vibration, leaving JBE with no alternative but to remove the rotors and ship them back to GE for further examination and repair. As a consequence, the project fell behind schedule and the client, having incurred heavy penalties by being unable to satisfy its own contract with its customer, invoked the liquidated damages provision of the contract.

Despite it later being shown that the turbines had a design flaw, the amount payable by GE to JBE was only a fraction of the penalties imposed by KPL, and left JBE facing a massive claim for damages. On top of this, the major sub-contractors - seeking payment for the steam turbine generators, and generators, supplied for the project - then (unsuccessfully) sued the company. The magnitude of the Keadby fiasco started to become apparent in early 1995 and, along with other problems, contributed significantly to the demise of Trafalgar House.

The post-Keadby Era

The losses on the Keadby contract were compounded by further losses on other major contracts. One such was the Kemsley Mill turnkey project in Kent. This was awarded by PowerGen Limited to JBE in November 1993, and covered the design, engineering and construction of a combined cycle heat and power (CHP) plant to replace the existing steam generating plant which was using 5,000 tons of coal per week. Central to the project was a JBE-built Frame 6 gas turbine which, together with two WHRBs, supplied the steam for three paper mills on site, plus a fourth at Sittingbourne. In addition to powering the mills, the system fed surplus power into the regional electricity grid in a deal with Grovehurst Energy Limited. Although this contract was successfully completed, unfortunately JBE suffered a substantial financial loss, due in the main to a lack of sufficient resources in the early days of the project.

By 1995, all Trafalgar House's problems started to come home, and this was never more true than in the case of a Clydebank facility still reeling from the grievous loss of former Managing Director, Graham Strachan, who died in a fire on New Year's Day. The de-rated

Keadby Power Station was ultimately handed over to KPL at the end of January 1996, one year later than agreed; both the paper mill combined cycle plants at Aylesford and Kemsley Mill were running late; there were major delays on several of the water and sewerage contracts, and the Salt Union combined cycle plant for Scottish Hydro-Electric was also getting into difficulties. Keadby's problems were generally considered to be largely the responsibility of GE, and this coincided with a perception that GE's attitude to its MAs had become less supportive. Apart from the insufficiency of the manning levels as the company wrestled with its biggest ever order book, there were arguably also problems in certain areas within the company. Despite the valiant efforts of many who worked endlessly through nights and weekends to try to keep the projects on schedule, the reality was that the company was never going to be able to do so. Nobody within JBE, however, believed for one moment that their problems would be such that a profit of £8m in 1994 would be transformed to a loss of £66m in 1995. As a consequence of JBE's, and others, difficulties, Trafalgar House's trading position slumped from a profit of £80m in 1994 to a loss of £108m in 1995, thus leaving the Group vulnerable to a take over bid yet again.

i   Dunbar, Charles (1984), "Crash diet gives John Brown new life", Report of the Week, journal name unknown, 6 September (from JBE Press Cutting file *What the papers say*).
ii   John Brown Engineering Limited (n.d.), *ATP and the Chinese Power Station Contracts won by JBE Limited in 1986: An Analysis of UK Benefits*, Clydebank: John Brown Engineering Limited.
iii   *Daily Express* (1988), 17 November, p2.
iv   *Evening Times* (1988), 17 November, p20.
v   *Evening Times* (1988), 17 November, p20.
vi   *John Brown Panorama* (1990), Spring.
vii   *Trafalgar House News* (1992), September/October, p1.
viii   *Glasgow Herald* (1993), 15 December, p16.

10 The Kvaerner Era

Kvaerner takes over at the Helm
The anticipated take-over bid for the financially stricken Trafalgar House duly came midway through 1995, when Kvaerner's Erik Tonseth offered to buy Trafalgar House's Engineering and Construction Division.

Tonseth, whose aggressive acquisition policies were once parodied in a Norwegian magazine article with the comment "Mr Tonseth hasn't bought anything this week!",[i] was President of the Norwegian conglomerate, Kvaerner AS. In ten years, this businessman had transformed a largely Norwegian company employing almost 10,000 employees, into a multinational company employing five times as many. Established in 1814, it had been one of the first GE MAs. In the late 1980s and early 1990s Tonseth had continued the rapid expansion of Kvaerner's shipbuilding interests by acquiring new shipyards throughout the world, including (in 1988) British Shipbuilders Govan Yard (later Kvaerner Govan). This more than any other acquisition was responsible for transforming the company into a significant multinational. After a 1990 merger with Thune Eureka, Kvaerner Energy AS was formed in 1992. By then shipbuilding (although the largest and most profitable sector) was only one of Kvaerner's six core activities, the others being shipping, metals, pulp and paper, hydropower, and oil and gas. Kvaerner believed that the acquisition of Trafalgar House's Engineering and Construction Division would strengthen some of these activities. However, despite having posted losses of £320m in 1995, Trafalgar House initially turned down the Kvaerner offer. In early 1996, however, after Tonseth had unsuccessfully attempted to take control of UK construction group, Amec, he renewed his interest in Trafalgar House, making a second offer - on this occasion for the entire Group. This £904m bid in February 1996 was a Norwegian acquisition record, attracted the support of major shareholders, such as Hongkong Land, and was successful.

The formal take-over, likened by some to Trafalgar House "hauling down its ensign",[ii] came into effect on 14 April 1996. Kvaerner were now effectively one of the largest oil and gas fabrication and construction companies in the world, with significant potential for future expansion in the fast growing Far East markets, where Trafalgar House's construction and contracting expertise was already well-established.

The acquisition was not, however, without its problems. Before the company could reap the rewards of its greater size, it was obliged to undergo a period of change and rationalisation, due to debts inherited by Kvaerner as a result of the acquisition. On the management side, the first casualty was Nigel Rich, who stepped down as Chief Executive, in favour of Erik Tonseth. Non-core businesses, which did not neatly fit into Kvaerner's portfolio of interests, were quickly identified and sold off to reduce the debts: this included prestigious names, such as London's Ritz Hotel and Cunard. By May 1997 the company had identified and sold assets worth $1bn, in addition to identifying further saleable assets which would achieve another $400m by April 1998.

A further consequence of the take-over was the need to standardise conditions and practices throughout the expanded Group. To achieve this, Kvaerner officials gave themselves one hundred days in which to familiarise themselves with all the Trafalgar House subsidiaries. Accordingly, by July 1996 the restructuring and unification process was already well under way. One important change was the replacement of Trafalgar House Group's company names and logos with that of Kvaerner in order, it was said, to "create a sense of community"[iii] and emphasise the size and strength of the company.

Despite the rapid implementation of the rationalisation exercise, however, Kvaerner's improved financial state in 1997 was still poorer than Tonseth had anticipated. In particular, Kvaerner Energy, Norway (KEN) had been expected to return to profit in 1998, but instead had performed poorly. This dragged down profits from the more lucrative shipbuilding arm. Despite remedial measures being taken throughout the whole Group during the early part of 1998, the financial position remained basically unchanged. By October speculation was mounting that Asea Brown Boveri (ABB) Director, Kjell Erik Almskog, would replace Tonseth as Group President and Chief Executive Officer, should Tonseth be forced to step down. This became a reality in October 1998, and on 1 January 1999 Almskog officially took over as President and Chief Executive Officer. He immediately decided to halt further expansion, and instead concentrate on consolidating the activities of the company as it stood. Significantly for Clydebank, he asserted that, while everyone would be given an opportunity to prove their worth, nothing was sacred: particularly non-core businesses, or companies unlikely to return to profitability in the short term.[iv]

While local reaction to the take over of Trafalgar House was generally favourable, the aftermath of Keadby left Clydebank management with more pressing problems. These problems had been further compounded in early 1996 by the resignations of Managing Director, Raymond McCabe, and all but one of the senior Directors. Although John Brown Engineering & Constructors' Chief Executive, Derek Hanson, temporarily filled the gap left by Raymond McCabe, the resolution of the Operations Division's massive liabilities (including claims from customers, sub-contractors and even partners) largely fell to the remaining Director, Chris Packard. Latterly, in addition to running CSD, Chris Packard had taken responsibility for International Sales. He was appointed JBE's new Managing Director in July 1996. With the assistance of Kvaerner's legal staff in London, and individuals such as Tommy Rae, Donald Beveridge and Project Manager, John Thomson (who

Chris Packard, President KEL, 1996 - 2001

largely resolved the water and sewerage problems), Chris was able to resolve the majority of the outstanding claims by a combination of negotiation and litigation. The resolution of outstanding problems at Keadby was largely due to Power Projects Director, Alex Crawford, who worked on the project on an almost full-time basis for a period of over two years. In addition to the resolution of all outstanding claims, one of the first visible effects of Kvaerner's acquisition of Trafalgar House was JBE's change of name to Kvaerner Energy Limited (KEL). Although seemingly a minor issue at main board level (and in line with the stated objective to standardise logos throughout the Group), there were many within the industry generally, and JBE specifically, who felt strongly that the loss of a much-respected name was a poor strategic decision. These feelings were echoed within the local community and by local politicians. A further effect was the loss of a significant number of jobs - despite Tonseth's initial assurance that there would be few redundancies.

Other changes followed. In July 1996 for example, a new company, Kvaerner Thermal Power (KTP), was formed out of a merger of KEL and Kvaerner Thermal Power Norway (KTN). The new company had five Divisions, three in Clydebank's KEL (Manufacturing, Services, and Power Projects) and two in Norway's KTN (one of which manufactured aero-derivative GE turbines). In April 1997, in an increasingly competitive market where new orders were proving hard to find, and with the parent Group requesting KTP find savings of £32m, KTP announced a partial re-structuring. It was hoped that this re-structuring would restore their competitive edge and result in much needed new orders for the Manufacturing Division, but the immediate result was the loss of a further 137 jobs at Clydebank. By 6 November 1998, with a collapsing Asian market, and a combination of weak oil prices and high sterling costs, the KEL operations were again rationalised. Management had no choice but to inform the 790 strong workforce at Clydebank that seventy-five further jobs would be lost, with more to follow should there be no improvement in the company's trading position.

Business as usual
Despite the constant fear that Kvaerner (like Trafalgar House before it) was intent on selling-off the loss-making KTP, and the attendant uncertainties, KEL still managed to secure orders throughout the late 1990s. Amongst these was the replacement of a Clydebank-built Frame 6 gas turbine for the Kipevu Thermal Power Station in Mombassa. Following an urgent telephone call from the Kenya Power & Lighting Company for a replacement turbine, this was flown out of Prestwick Airport to Mombassa on a giant Russian Antonov freighter, and duly installed on site - all within the space of fifty-two days! The faulty turbine was left on

Flying out the Kipevu replacement gas turbine from Prestwick Airport

Chris Packard with Cuban President, Fidel Castro, at the opening of Valedaro Power Station

site but two years later (now somewhat rusty) was shipped back to Clydebank for refurbishment, and later re-installed in Mombassa to meet an increased demand for power!

Other major contracts won at this time included one for the supply of two Frame 5 mechanical drive units for the Sonatrach Tin Fouye Tabankort Gas Field in South East Algeria, and three for the supply of five Frame 6 gas turbines for Cuba. These latter contracts were brokered via the Sherritt Power Corporation in Canada, because of political sensitivities between America and Cuba. Further contracts included the supply of Frame 6 gas turbines and associated equipment for the French company, COFIVA, and a $40m turnkey project in the United Arab Emirates. This latter contract for the construction of a

Frame 6 gas turbines destined for China: the different coloured tarpaulins indicated which power station they were destined for

70mw power station (JBE's sixty-fourth gas turbine for the UAE), was placed by the Abu Dhabi Company for Onshore Oil Operations. Powered by two Clydebank-built Frame 6 gas turbines, it utilised the latest Dry Low NOx technology for reducing emissions. In 1999, JBE also completed the work on what was their last Chinese contract: the gas and steam combined cycle power station at Zhenhai.

KEL's final major contract was from the Oil and Natural Gas Corporation in India. This was for the refurbishment of three LM2500 gas turbines for an oil platform operating at the Bombay High South Offshore Complex, sited approximately 160 kilometres off the west coast of India. It was, according to Project Manager Ian Deans, unlike anything that had gone before. Under the contract, KEL was responsible for all overall design and procurement work, and the pre-engineering, fabrication and transportation of equipment. The latter involved the shipping out of all materials, firstly to Bombay Port, and then onwards to the platform itself. Once on board, KEL was responsible for the de-hooking and re-installation

ONGC oil platform, Bombay High South Offshore complex

of the existing gas turbines. The necessity for the client's operations to continue while the refurbishment was taking place, plus the remoteness of the site, the occurrence of monsoons and serious concerns for safety, made work on this project particularly difficult - to say the least! These difficulties were made worse on one occasion when oil slicks, which were floating around the base of one of the platform structures, were inadvertently set alight, giving rise to sixty-foot high flames and causing the evacuation of everyone from the oil platform.

KEL goes Up for Sale

On 13 April 1999, after months of rumours, Scottish industry was stunned when, following a major re-evaluation of the Group's global activities, it was confirmed that Kvaerner was selling the Govan Shipyard and KEL. A corporate decision had been taken to withdraw from a number of fields, including shipbuilding and thermal power. The 'new Kvaerner' thus created was a slimmed down version of the former company with only three core activities: oil and

Evening Times headline, 1999
Reproduced courtesy of The Herald and Evening Times. Copyright of Newsquest Media Group

gas; engineering and construction; and construction (building and civil engineering).

However unwelcome, the decision came as no surprise to the Clydebank management. Since the take-over of Trafalgar House three years previously, they had been fighting unsuccessfully to establish KEL as a core business within the Group. Predictably the announcement created a media storm, and pressure was immediately put on the parent company by both the Scottish Executive, and the Scottish trade union movement, to rescind the decision.

On the day Kvaerner announced they were selling KEL and the Govan Shipyard, a four-man Task Force was set up by Lord Macdonald, the Scottish Industry Minister. They were charged with trying to convince Kvaerner not to sell the two facilities, and, if this failed, to

STUC boss Bill Speirs with Clydebank Trades Council officials handing over a 6,000 names petition during the fight to save KEL

identify a 'white knight' to take over the two facilities. Former 'Bankie',[v] and Amalgamated Engineering and Electrical Union (AEEU) General Secretary, Sir Gavin Laird, was appointed Chairman of this Task Force. The other members were the prominent Scottish businessmen Malcolm Clark, Bill Scott and David Smith. Although the sale of Govan shipyard attracted most of the media attention, this was partly because the Clydebank management (and local Unions) were confident that a buyer would be found for the Clydebank facility. Indeed, it was thought that publicity might scare off potential buyers. However, in the event, the shipyard proved the easier of the two to sell, with BAE Systems formally taking it over on 15 December 1999.

Initially Kvaerner had agreed to sell its Thermal Power Division as a single entity, and a working committee was formed to ensure that this commitment was honoured. The committee, comprising local politicians, job creation agencies and representatives of the KEL Unions, hoped that they would thus prevent any asset-stripping of the Clydebank company. In July 1999 an *Information Memorandum*[vi] was circulated to approximately 500 companies, seeking potential buyers for the Thermal Power Division, which at this stage comprised KEL in Clydebank and KTN in Norway. Both were still headed by Chris Packard, and supported three Divisions (Manufacturing, Services and Power Projects) in Clydebank, and three Divisions (Power Systems, Repairs & Maintenance, and Small Gas Turbines) in Norway. Also to be included in the sale was a 49 per cent share in Masaood John Brown. At that time, KEL was in a reasonably healthy financial state, with Power Projects bidding for six major contracts worth approximately £200m, and Services Division holding an order book valued at £55m.

Following the circulation of the *Information Memorandum*, a shortlist of approximately ten interested companies was drawn up. However, on 2 September 1999 (one day before offers closed) a late bid, in the form of a letter of intent, was received from GE. This was only for KEL's Power Projects and Services Divisions, plus KTN in Norway, and was also conditional on Kvaerner abandoning the open bidding process it had recently embarked upon to find a potential buyer. Although the bid was somewhat unexpected at the time, it was in accordance with GE's strategy over recent years of taking over or closing down, its former MAs. In this case, it would allow GE to acquire KEL's customer base, along with potential repeat orders for spares, service, and operations and maintenance contracts. In the event, the GE bid was successful and was formally accepted by Kvaerner on 27 December 1999. In total GE paid Kvaerner approximately $70m. The transfer to GE's payroll of the 430 staff employed within Power Projects and Services Divisions of KEL took place at the end of March 2000. They remained in their existing office accommodation on Glasgow Road, Clydebank, under a short-term leasing agreement with Kvaerner until the summer of 2002, when they re-located to offices in Glasgow.

The Beginning of the End

Inevitably, the sale had left the Manufacturing Division weaker and somewhat exposed - something bitterly resented by those employed within this Division. However, GE's refusal to take over KEL's Manufacturing Division was entirely predictable for, with a sufficiency of manufacturing capability in their existing plants, the outdated and now

Robbie Robertson, KEL Shop Stewards Convener, addressing the workforce, 1999

unsuitable Clydebank facility was seen as more of a liability than an asset.

Once the GE bid had been accepted, the only alternative to closure of the Manufacturing Division was to either encourage a Management Buy Out (MBO) by the existing Clydebank management, or find an independent purchaser for the remaining Division. With only scant interest in the market place, the former option was subsequently pursued by Chris Packard, Stuart Queen and Steve Nesbit. Their first offer appeared initially to be well received by the Kvaerner Board. They proposed to maintain the Clydebank Works for a period of four years to enable them to reduce costs, thereby improving efficiency, and thus return the Division to profitability. As November turned to early December, Chris Packard went to discuss the proposal with Almskog, whilst at the same time submitting an RSA Grant Application for additional funding to the Scottish Executive. Although a verbal agreement was reached with the Kvaerner Board in respect of the main issues and pre-conditions (including a verbally agreed three year work commitment from GE), two issues proved to be a stumbling block: site contamination and financial support. The level of financial support was crucial to the bid and included, in addition to the RSA grant, a £3.5m payment by Kvaerner and a $3m loan from GE. Assuming all MBO pre-conditions were met by 10 December, Chris Packard was confident the new company could be operational by 6 January 2000. However, ultimately this bid, and two further revised bids, were rejected by Almskog.

At the beginning of December, the failure of the MBO bid, and the consequent probable loss of approximately three hundred jobs, was greeted locally with dismay. Shortly afterwards it was announced that the Manufacturing Division would close once all outstanding work was completed, unless a new buyer could be found. Kvaerner agreed a stay of execution for twelve months.

This decision was particularly bitterly received by the workforce, who believed that there was sufficient work to keep the 272 workers fully occupied for the foreseeable future, but agreed to co-operate in the search for a new owner. Whilst this belief may have been correct, unfortunately the reality was that since the 1996 take-over the Manufacturing Division had incurred annual losses of over £1m, due to a failure to achieve targeted production levels. Although its core business was still the manufacture of Frame 5, 6 and 9E gas turbines, it had, in 1998, completed only six Frame 6 turbines: a far cry from the days when it produced almost one gas turbine per week. Also, while the Power Projects Division in Clydebank was still able to secure major contracts during the late 1990s, the majority of the gas turbines required to fulfil these contracts were not manufactured in Clydebank, but supplied by GE or other MAs. This was partly a consequence of the Manufacturing Division's loss of competitiveness, but mostly due to the abandonment (except for Frame 6 gas turbines) of their much vaunted Advance Ordering programme. A further change sprang from a deliberate policy (encouraged by GE) to undertake the manufacture of a range of less profitable gas turbine components including casings, exhausts and base frames, primarily for GE and also other clients, such as Alsthom. This was essentially sub-contracting work and, while it may initially have been seen as a means of supplementing gas turbine orders, by the late 1990s it provided 80 per cent of the Division's revenue generating activity.

In July 1999 (when the *Information Memorandum* was circulated) there had been two unsold Frame 6 gas turbines in stock, and a further three in the process of manufacture. In effect the last gas turbine contract was placed on 12 November 1999 by the Canadian Sherritt Corporation. From then, until closure in March 2001, the Manufacturing Division were exclusively engaged in the manufacture of gas turbine components. In order to reduce the rates burden (and thus operating costs), the Fabrication Works were eventually closed and all fabrication work was concentrated in Bay 11 of the Engine Works.

In February 2000, the *Information Memorandum* was re-issued to several interested parties, including the Harker Group, the C.W. Cook Group, and the Texas Group. With several of these having already visited, or proposing to visit the Works, Chris Packard had every reason to be hopeful that the future of the Works could be secured. A fourth bid came from former JBE Sales Director, Bob Hepburn, heading a consortium (provisionally called Newco) of ex-JBE managers, who renewed an earlier interest. Ultimately, it was the Texas Group which gained 'preferred bidder' status.

Around April 2000 a Draft Agreement between Texas and Kvaerner was prepared. However, on 5 July, with the finish line in sight, Texas withdrew without specifying their reasons. It was later alleged that it may have been due to a seven day 'work in' (prompted by concerns over pension and redundancy rights)[vii] by the remaining workers. During this work-in, workers continued to take instructions from foremen and middle management, but used equipment such as forklift trucks to deny shop floor access to everyone else. This allegation was dismissed by Texas, who claimed that an agreement of these issues had in fact been reached months earlier, in December 1999.

Although Texas had withdrawn, Bob Hepburn remained interested in buying the Manufacturing Division. He had met with Kvaerner management in June 2000, and initially the bid appeared to be satisfactory, with Bob able to confirm sufficient financial backing. As a former JBE Sales Director, he was also able to satisfy the local Unions. In fact, his previous knowledge of the Works and strong GE contacts were particularly attractive to the workforce.

Although a preliminary agreement was reached with Bob Hepburn's consortium on 7 November 2000, Kvaerner later reported that they had failed to reach an agreement, citing financial concerns and difficulties in obtaining a waiver from the Scottish Executive for possible site contamination penalties. On 16 November 2000 Kvaerner announced that, as Newco could not satisfy the conditions of the preliminary agreement, they had reluctantly decided to terminate the discussions. Further (and despite a last minute appeal, and the promise of generous financial assistance, from the Scottish Executive's Wendy Alexander), Kvaerner re-affirmed its intention to close the Clydebank Works.

The collapse of yet another bid prompted local MSP Des McNulty to allege years of under-investment by both Trafalgar House and Kvaerner. The decision by Kvaerner to close the Clydebank Works, he said, was a "devastating blow for the workforce and the town".[viii] He was particularly angry that, despite much lobbying by himself and others, Kvaerner had pulled out of negotiations just when he felt they were on the verge of securing a deal to take over the manufacturing side of the business.

The news of the collapse of the negotiations with Newco was treated with resignation and little surprise. In realising that there was now no alternative to closure, both management and Unions agreed a final exit plan, but continued to work together until the final contract was completed, one week ahead of schedule. The final weeks of one of the world's greatest shipyards had been conducted with dignity. KEL's last Shop Steward Convener, Robbie Robertson said, however, that it was the end of "100 years history in Clydebank".[ix] *The Herald* stated that it was the "end of an era"[x] when 200 workers clocked out of the Kvaerner Energy plant in Clydebank for the last time in March 2001. All that remained was a small nucleus of men to look after and maintain the site and buildings.

On 14 May 2001, however, it was reported that Texas had renewed its interest in buying the site and buildings and, again, had been granted 'preferred' bidder status. This was subsequently confirmed, and negotiations recommenced, with the intention that an eventual sale be completed by 6 June 2001. Despite further site visits by Texas personnel, by 26 June 2001 the deal had still not been completed. The major problem was that of access: main access to the Works was from Cart Street, which was wholly within the boundary of the former Shipyard occupied by UIE. Consequently, for the final time Texas withdrew.

Fresh negotiations then commenced with a syndicate called Clydeside Regeneration Limited. At the same time, on Thursday 21 June 2001, it was announced that the adjoining former shipyard site was up for sale, and this was acquired by Clydeside Regeneration Limited. Finally on Friday morning, 12 October 2001, the syndicate also bought the Kvaerner site. By the late summer of 2002, the Clydebank site was in the process of being cleared.

---

i   Hagen, Sturle (1996), "An Industrial Crusader", *Kvaerner Focus*, No.2, September, pp8-9.
ii   *Glasgow Herald* (1996), 5 March, p23.
iii   *Kvaerner Focus* (1996), No.1, July, p2.
iv   *Kvaerner Focus* (1998), November, p2.
v   Someone born in Clydebank.
vi   PricewaterhouseCoopers (1999), *Information Memorandum*, July.
vii   In actual fact, in November 2000 a Negotiating Committee (comprising representatives of GMB, MSF, AEEU and ACATT) and a Management Negotiating Team of Chris Packard, Jack Findlay and Steve Griffen, ratified the agreement on pensions and redundancy, valid for one year from 21 December 1999, or until such time as a buyer for the company could be found.
viii *Clydebank Post* (2000), 23 November, p4.
ix   *Evening Times* (2000), 17 November, p6.
x   *The Herald* (2000), 23 December, p4.

11   Conclusion

Objectively viewed, despite ultimately gaining a well-deserved reputation in terms of the size and number of contracts gained, JBE was never a major league player in the power generation industry. Whilst in a good year, GE and its MAs might get 60 per cent of the world market in gas turbine manufacture, JBE alone could, at best, look for no more than between 6 and 8 per cent. After the shipbuilding side was nationalised, the company may have lost a lot of its glamour, but its achievements in the gas turbine field remain outstanding and equally worthy of attention.

JBE's success can be attributed to various factors, but none more so than the decision to enter into an MA Agreement with GE, giving the company access to the best and most modern gas turbine technology in the world, and enabling JBE to capitalise on a world-wide market desperate for power generation plant. In itself, however, this does not fully explain how a relatively small Scottish company lacking financial muscle was able to take on and beat much bigger competitors, and penetrate difficult markets such as China, the USSR, Burma and Iraq, which for many years were closed to outside businesses. Many explain this success by pointing to three other significant factors. Firstly, the company's willingness (ironically, made possible by its relative lack of size) to offer potential clients a customised product at a competitive price. In effect, JBE could tailor its products to client's specification. Added to this was the persistence of a local management team that, when pursuing a contract, was never prepared to admit defeat, and moved heaven and earth to win the order! Secondly, by having the courage to maintain an Advance Order programme in good times and bad, JBE was able to offer clients a far quicker delivery time. In contracts such as the Bahamas and Kenya, where speed was essential, this factor alone was often sufficient to secure the contract. Thirdly, was JBE's ingenuity once the contract had been won in resolving difficulties as they arose. Sometimes, as in the case of the Russian pipeline orders (where the turbines had to be very carefully crated to enable them to negotiate the narrow railway tunnels), the difficulties were resolved in Clydebank, but often problems were resolved by field employees armed only with a good dose of common sense and typical Clydeside humour!

Despite the commendably few disappointing contracts, the Clydebank management successfully negotiated the company through over forty years of outstanding achievement, thereby adding greatly to the legend of Clydeside. JBE outlived many of its rivals, and fellow MAs, and demonstrated on several occasions that it was indeed the brightest 'jewel', not only among GE's 'string of pearls', but within the parent company itself!

Indeed, the importance of the quality of management and workers which JBE drew upon, cannot be over-emphasised. At the pinnacle were the four Managing Directors who each, in their different ways, gave direction and leadership to the company during widely differing market conditions. To George and Graham Strachan fell the task of transforming a lacklustre Engine Works into a forward-looking gas turbine manufacturer and, thereafter, guiding the new entity through its formative years. Raymond McCabe had the task of re-invigorating the company after the dark days of the early 1980s, when it was on its knees, and thereafter re-shaping it to meet the challenges of new and changing markets. Finally, Chris Packard oversaw the dignified demise of the company in its final difficult years. Under these four individuals, the company benefited from a management that lived for the company.

As for the workers, one former Managing Director asserted they "defied gravity"! In the last resort it was the men and women - especially the site personnel - who were called upon to work in the coldest and hottest environments in the world, away from their homes and families, who gave the company its well-deserved reputation. Sometimes caught up in local riots, unrest or outright war, their's was not an easy task. In the early 1970s, for example, while working on one of the Burmese contracts, rebel soldiers lobbed mortars into a compound being used by JBE personnel, and again in the early 1980s JBE employees were several times caught up in enemy attacks on Iraqi installations during the Iraq-Iran war. JBE site staff were applauded by their Chinese hosts when they were among the first Westerners to return to Beijing after the 1989 Tiananmen Square massacre to resume work on vital power station contracts.

While, inevitably, there was anger within the local community at the loss of this local industry, JBE perhaps survived longer than might have initially been thought possible. Life does not stand still, and this is especially true of industry. The situation forty years ago was markedly different than today. Then, companies such as JBE could still hope to pick up work from Commonwealth countries and former colonies; many economies, especially in the Middle and Far East, bolstered by huge oil revenues, could afford to embark on hugely ambitious power generation projects. JBE found itself operating in a very competitive and cyclical industry where one year's feast could easily be followed by several years of famine.

A further difficulty was that JBE did not own the technology required to manufacture gas turbines. Throughout its existence, JBE was completely reliant on the goodwill of GE to make this technology available to the company. Up until the early 1990s, the links that existed between GE and its MAs ensured that this was not a problem, but thereafter these links were weakened as GE began to embark on a programme to either take over or close down MAs.

It was, however, the massive losses from high risk contracts such as Keadby that ultimately led to JBE's decline. Furthermore, after Keadby the Group would not permit JBE to tender for high risk contracts, or carry out a full Advance Order programme. These measures, whilst ensuring there were no further major loss-making contracts at Clydebank, equally meant that new orders were hard to come by.

The final nail in the coffin, however, was the fact that, although Clydebank's financial performance under Kvaerner was positive, problems with the Norwegian arm of the business prevented it being seen by Kvaerner as a core business.

Ultimately, how will history judge JBE? Probably with astonishment that so small an enterprise could make so much of an impact on a fiercely competitive and risky environment. Perhaps the legacy of the last Managing Director, Chris Packard, was to give the community of Clydebank, and the workforce, a much needed breathing space in which to come to terms with the loss of Clydebank's last great industrial enterprise, and the consolation that, in commissioning this book, he ensured that (as he put it) the "last chapter could be written".

Milestones for John Brown Engineering

Date	Description
1965, May	Signing of Manufacturing Associate Agreement with General Electric Company
1966, October	Formation of John Brown Engineering (Clydebank) Limited
1967, June	First JBE-built gas turbine shipped out to America for the Illinois Power Company
1968, November	First Middle East gas turbine order won
1970, April	JBE wins the first of six Queens Awards for Export Achievement
1971, December	First order from People's Republic of China
1974, August	First order from Soviet Union for Bratsvo oil pipeline
1976, August	£35m order from British Smelter Constructions - largest single order to date
1982, June	Imposition of embargo on Russian pipeline project by US President Ronald Reagan
1986, April	John Brown & Company Limited taken over by Trafalgar House plc
1989, June	JBE design and build first UK power station to run on North Sea gas
1991	JBE secures world's largest gas turbine order placed by Marubeni Corporation and destined for Iran
1992, April	JBE receive order to design and build world's first combined cycle power station utilising Frame 9F gas turbines
1996, April	Trafalgar House plc taken over by Kvaerner AS of Norway
1999, April	Kvaerner announce sale of KEL
1999, December	KEL's Power Projects and Services Divisions acquired by GE
2001, March	Gas turbine manufacture at Clydebank ceases with the closure of KEL Manufacturing Division
2001, October	Buildings and site acquired by Clydeside Regeneration Limited

List of Gas Turbine Contracts undertaken by John Brown Engineering

MS3002   Mechanical Drive

Customer	Country	Number Ordered	Total Rating HP	Fuel	Cycle	Order Date
GE for Esso	Australia	2	18600	Gas	SC	1968
GE for Esso	Australia	1	9300	Gas	SC	1969
GE for Tennessee Gas	USA	1	9300	Gas	SC	1970
GE/Michigan Wisconsin Pipeline Co.	USA	2	18600	Gas	RC	1970
Alsthom for SONATRACH	Algeria	1	9300	Gas	SC	1970
Qatar Petroleum Company	Qatar	7	98000	Gas	SC	1972
Phillips Petroleum	England	2	28000	Gas	SC	1972
C.J.B. for SONATRACH	Algeria	8	112000	Gas	SC	1973
GE for Exxon	Australia	2	18600	Gas	SC	1973
GE for Phillips Petroleum (Eldfisk)	North Sea	2	28000	Gas	SC	1974
Willbros for SONATRACH	Algeria	12	168000	Gas	SC	1974
GE for V/O Machinoimport	USSR	12	168000	Gas	SC	1974
AEG-Kanis for V/O Machinoimport	USSR	33	462000	Gas	SC	1976
P.S.M.E. for Q.P.P.A.	Qatar	1	14600	Gas	SC	1980
Thomassen for Shell	Nigeria	2	29200	Gas	SC	1980
V/O Machinoimport	USSR	1	14600	Gas	SC	1981
V/O Machinoimport	USSR	1	14600	Gas	SC	1982
Total		**90**	**1220700**			

MS5001   Mechanical Drive

Customer	Country	Number Ordered	Total Rating HP	Fuel	Cycle	Order Date
Arabian American Oil Company	Saudi Arabia	1	19800	Gas	SC	1967
GE for Alberta Natural Gas	Canada	1	16800	Gas	SC	1968
Total		**2**	**36600**			

MS5002   Mechanical Drive

Customer	Country	Number Ordered	Total Rating HP	Fuel	Cycle	Order Date
Hilmar Reksten	GTS "Lucian"	1	25000	Triple	RC	1974
Phillips Petroleum Co. Norway	Ekofisk Central	2	70000	Gas	SC	1974
Phillips Petroleum Co. Norway	South Eldfisk	2	70000	Gas	SC	1974
Phillips Petroleum Co. Norway	North Sea/EmdenPipeline	1	35000	Gas	SC	1975
Phillips Petroleum Co. Norway	North Sea/EmdenPipeline	2	70000	Gas	SC	1976
Nuovo Pignone for SONATRACH	Algeria	4	129000	Gas	SC	1976
Techimport	PRC	1	32250	Gas	SC	1976
Ralph M Parsons for Shell Expro	Scotland	2	64500	Gas	SC	1976
Fish Intl./Alberta Natural Gas	Canada	1	33000	Gas	HR	1977
De Laval Stork for ADNOC	Abu Dhabi	1	33550	Gas	SC	1978
Mitsubishi for SONATRACH	Algeria	3	105000	Gas	SC	1981
Lummus/Esso Chemical Ltd	Scotland	1	35000	Gas	RC	1981
V/O Machinoimport/MAB-Creusot-Loire	USSR	21	735000	Gas	HR	1981
N.C.C. for ARAMCO	Saudi Arabia	1	38000	Gas	SC	1993
B&R/Sulzer - SONATRACH	Algeria	2	76000	Gas	SC	1996
Total		**45**	**1551300**			

MS3002   Power Generation

Customer	Country	Number Ordered	Total Rating kW	Fuel	Cycle	Order Date
GEC Elliott/Union Steamship Co.	New Zealand	1	* 9000	Dist	RC	1972
Bechtel for BP	Das. Is., Abu Dhabi	2	20000	Gas	SC	1973
Conoco UK	England	1	10000	Dual	HR	1979
Total		**4**	**39000**			

* Part of marine propulsion package

MS5001   Power Generation

Customer	Country	Number Ordered	Total Rating kW	Fuel	Cycle	Order Date
GE for Connecticut Light & Power	USA	1	16000	Dist	SC	1967
GE for Illinois Power Company	USA	1	14000	Dist	SC	1967
GE for Missouri Power & Light	USA	1	14000	Gas	SC	1967
GE for Instituto Nacional De Elect.	Guatemala	1	14000	Dist	SC	1967
GE for Commonwealth Edison	USA	4	63000	Dual	SC	1968
Yanhee Electricity Authority	Thailand	2	29500	Dist	SC	1968
Ministry of Water & Electricity (1&2)	Abu Dhabi	2	29900	Dual	SC	1968
GE for Commonwealth Edison	USA	1	15750	Dual	SC	1968
Brunei Electricity Authority	Brunei	1	11000	Gas	SC	1968
British Smelter Constr. Ltd (1-9)	Bahrain	9	137250	Dual	SC	1968
Ministry of Water & Electricity (3-5)	Abu Dhabi	3	44880	Dual	DS	1968
Yanhee Electricity Authority	Thailand	2	29500	Gas	SC	1968
GE for Commonwealth Edison	USA	3	44250	Dual	SC	1968
GE for Consolidated Edison	USA	1	15250	Dual	SC	1968
British Smelter Constr. Ltd (10-14)	Bahrain	5	76250	Dual	SC	1969
Puerto Rico Water Resources Auth	Puerto Rico	6	122550	Gas	SC	1969
Bahamas Electricity Corporation (1)	Bahamas	1	14750	Dist	SC	1969
GE for Iberduero	Spain	1	15250	Dist	SC	1969
Bahamas Electricity Corporation (2)	Bahamas	1	14750	Dist	SC	1969
GE for Dayton Power & Light	USA	2	30500	Dual	SC	1969
GE for Consolidated Edison	USA	1	15250	Dual	SC	1969
GE for Carolina Power & Light	USA	4	61000	Dual	SC	1970
GE for BP Alaska Inc.	USA	2	30500	Gas	SC	1970
GE for Virginia Electric Power Co.	USA	1	15250	Dist	SC	1970
Bahamas Electricity Corporation (3)	Bahamas	1	14750	Dist	SC	1970
S.E.G.B.A.	Argentina	7	106750	Dist	SC	1970
British Smelter Constr. Ltd (15-18)	Bahrain	4	76400	Dual	SC	1970
Arabian American Oil Co.	Saudi Arabia	1	15250	Dual	SC	1970
China Light & Power Co Ltd	Hong Kong	1	18800	Residual	CC	1970
SONELGAZ	Algeria	3	56400	Gas	SC	1970
Turku Municipality Electricity Works	Finland	1	18800	Dist	SC	1970
State Energy Comm. of W. Australia	Australia	2	37600	Dist	SC	1970
GE for UNELCO	Canary Isles	1	15250	Dual	SC	1970
SONELGAZ	Algeria	2	37600	Gas	SC	1971
Agua Y Energia Electrica	Argentina	2	37600	Dist	SC	1971
Electricity Supply Board (1-3)	Burma	3	70200	Dist	SC	1971
China National Mach. Import & Export	PRC	5	114500	Dist	SC	1971
Ministry of Water & Electricity (6)	Abu Dhabi	1	26100	Dist	SC	1972
Hidro Electrica Do Alto Catumbela	Angola	1	23750	Dist	SC	1972
Public Power Corporation - Greece	Crete	2	32500	Dist	SC	1972
China National Mach. Import & Export	PRC	3	63000	Dual	SC	1972
GE for Smorgon Consolidated Inds.	Australia	1	22000	Dual	SC	1972
Maritime Electric	PE Island, Canada	1	25000	Dist	SC	1972
Bahamas Electricity Corporation (4)	Bahamas	1	18800	Dist	DS	1972

MS5001   Power Generation (cont.)

Customer	Country	Number Ordered	Total Rating kW	Fuel	Cycle	Order Date
Jamaica Public Service Company (1)	Jamaica	1	24000	Dist	SC	1972
PLN (1)	Indonesia	1	24000	Dist	SC	1972
British Smelter Constr. Ltd (19)	Bahrain	1	25000	Dual	SC	1972
Jamaica Public Service Co. (2&3)	Jamaica	2	48000	Dist	SC	1973
Power Gas - Harris for ADMA	Abu Dhabi	6	144000	Dual	SC	1973
Bechtel for Occidental (Piper Field)	North Sea	2	48000	Dual	SC	1973
Mobil Oil (Beryl "A")	North Sea	3	72000	Dual	SC	1973
PLN (2)	Indonesia	1	24000	Dist	SC	1973
Syrian Arab Republic	Syria	4	96000	Dist	SC	1973
Petromin	Saudi Arabia	1	24000	Dual	SC	1973
Smorgon Consolidated Inds.	Australia	1	24000	Dual	HR	1974
Ministry of Water & Electricity (7&8)	Abu Dhabi	2	48000	Dual	SC	1974
Ministry of Development & Eng. Serv.	Bahrain	2	48000	Gas	SC	1974
Dubai Electricity Co.	Dubai	1	24000	Dual	SC	1974
Matthew Hall for Occidental (Claymore)	North Sea	2	48000	Dual	SC	1974
Lummus for Chevron (Ninian)	North Sea	5	120000	Dual	HR	1974
Lummus/Crest for Chevron (Ninian)	North Sea	1	24000	Dual	SC	1974
PLN (3)	Indonesia	1	24000	Dist	SC	1975
Ministry of Water & Electricity (9&10)	Abu Dhabi	2	48000	Dual	SC	1975
Foster Wheeler for BP (1&2)	Shetland Isles	2	48000	Dual	HR	1975
BP	Das Island	1	24000	Gas	SC	1975
Trinidad & Tobago Electricity Comm.	Trinidad	2	48000	Gas	SC	1976
S.W.A.W.E.K.	S W Africa	1	24000	Dist	SC	1976
King Saud University	Saudi Arabia	4	96000	Dist	SC	1976
Penske for Fairbanks Municipality	Alaska	1	24000	Dual	SC	1976
Citizens Utilities Company	Kauai, Hawaii	1	24000	Dist	RP	1976
Water & Electricity Department	Al Ain	2	48000	Dual	SC	1976
H.S.P.E./Dubai Aluminium	Dubai	8	192000	Dual	DS	1976
Energia Electrica (1)	Venezuela	1	24000	Dual	SC	1976
Dubai Electricity Company	Dubai	3	72000	Dist	SC	1976
Thyssen-Lummus/Iraq National Refy.	Iraq	4	96000	Gas	SC	1976
Energia Electrica (2)	Venezuela	1	23000	Dual	SC	1976
Ministry of Electricity & Water	Ajman	2	48000	Dist	SC	1976
Foster Wheeler for BP (3&4)	Shetland Isles	2	48000	Dual	HR	1977
Trinidad & Tobago Electricity Comm.	Trinidad	2	48000	Gas	SC	1977
EPC (4&5)	Burma	2	48000	Dual	CC	1977
EPC (6)	Burma	1	24000	Dual	SC	1977
Pemex	Mexico	2	48000	Dual	SC	1977
Foster Wheeler for BP No. 5	Shetland Isles	1	24000	Dual	HR	1977
McDermott Hudson/Dubai Nat. Gas Co	Dubai	1	24000	Gas	SC	1978
Lummus for BP	Netherlands	2	48000	Dual	HR	1978
Technoimport	Vietnam	3	72000	Dual	SC	1978
West Bengal State Electricity Board	India	5	120000	Dist	SC	1978
KAE, Curacao	Neth. Antilles	1	24000	Dist	CC	1978
EPC (7-9)	Burma	3	72000	Dual	SC	1979
Slough Estates	England	1	24000	Gas/Res	RP	1979
Freeport Power Company	Bahamas	1	24000	Dist	SC	1979
Arabian Gulf Expl. Co.	Libya	2	48000	Dual	SC	1979
Aluminium Bahrain (20-24)	Bahrain	5	120000	Dual	SC	1979
Matthew Hall/BP (Magnus Field)	North Sea	1	24000	Dual	HR	1979

MS5001 Power Generation (cont.)

Customer	Country	Number Ordered	Total Rating kW	Fuel	Cycle	Order Date
Matthew Hall/BP (Magnus Field)	North Sea	2	48000	Dual	SC	1979
Ceylon Electricity Board	Sri Lanka	3	72000	Dist	SC	1979
Phillips Petroleum Co.	Ekofisk Riser, Norway	2	49300	Gas	SC	1979
Hindustan Fertiliser Corporation	India	1	24000	Dist	SC	1980
E.P.E.C.	Argentina	3	72000	Dual	SC	1980
Arabian Gulf Oil Company	Libya	2	48000	Dual	SC	1980
Brunei State Electrical Department	Brunei	4	96000	Gas	SC	1980
State Organisation of Electricity	Iraq	10	240000	Dual	SC	1981
Petroleum Development Oman	Oman	2	48000	Gas	SC	1981
BHEL for ONGC	India	2	48000	Gas	HR	1982
EPC (10)	Burma	1	24000	Dist/Res	SC	1982
EPC (11)	Burma	1	24000	Dual	SC	1982
EPC (12)	Burma	1	24000	Dist/Res	CC	1982
NEI for PUB	Singapore	2	50000	Dist	SC	1983
Hyundai/Misurata Steel	Libya	1	25000	Dist	SC	1984
Directorate of Electricity Services	Brunei	7	175000	Gas	HR	1984
Minenco Pty Ltd. for Hamersley Iron	Australia	1	25000	Dist	SC	1985
China National Mach. Import & Export	Hainan Is. PRC	2	50000	Dist/Crude	SC	1987
Liuzhou Zhen-Xing Power Co. Ltd	PRC	1	25000	Dist/HFO	SC	1988
B & R Vickers/Occidental (Piper)	North Sea	4	105000	Dual	HR	1989
NIOC	Iran	2	52000	Dual	SC	1990
BP Cusiana	Colombia	2	52000	Gas	SC	1995
BP Cusiana	Colombia	1	26000	Dual	SC	1995
BP Cupiogua	Colombia	2	52000	Dual	SC	1995
Total		**265**	**5727680**			

MS5002 Power Generation

Customer	Country	Number Ordered	Total Rating kW	Fuel	Cycle	Order Date
Trondheim Elektrisitetswerk	Trondheim	1	25400	Dist	CC	1979
Total		**1**	**25400**			

MS6001 Power Generation

Customer	Country	Number Ordered	Total Rating kW	Fuel	Cycle	Order Date
Water & Electricity Dept.	Abu Dhabi	4	140000	Dual	SC	1981
Micenco/Bougainville Copper Ltd	Papua New Guinea	2	70000	Dist	SC	1981
CFE	Mexico	2	70000	Dist	SC	1981
Bechtel for Esso Petroleum	England	1	35000	Dual	HR	1982
Thyssen/Kellog Pertamina	Indonesia	2	70000	Dual	HR	1983
Imperial Chemical Industries	England	1	35000	Gas	HR	1983
Saskatchewan Power Corporation	Canada	1	36000	Gas	SC	1984
Foster Wheeler for Tosco Refinery	USA	2	75000	Gas	HR	1985
NTEC	Australia	3	125000	Dual	SC	1985
NTEC	Australia	2	75000	Dual	CC	1985
Kenya Power & Lighting Co. Ltd	Kenya	1	37500	Dist	SC	1986
CNTIC for Ministry of Petroleum	PRC	2	75000	Gas	RP	1986
CNTIC for Ministry of Petroleum	PRC	1	37500	Gas	CC	1986
CNTIC for Ministry of Petroleum	PRC	2	75000	Gas	CC	1986
I.R.H.E.	Panama	2	75000	Dist	SC	1987
Huaneng Int. Power Dev. Corpn,	PRC	2	75000	Gas	CC	1988
O'Brien Energy for Newark Boxboard	USA	1	37500	Dual	CC	1988
O'Brien Energy for Dupont Parlin	USA	2	75000	Dual	CC	1988

MS6001 Power Generation (cont.)

Customer	Country	Number Ordered	Total Rating kW	Fuel	Cycle	Order Date
National Power Corporation	Philippines	5	187000	Dist	SC	1988
Nanning City GT Power Gen. Co.	PRC	1	37500	Dist	SC	1988
O.N.E.	Morocco	3	112500	Dist/Resid	SC	1989
Mount Isa Mines	Australia	1	37500	Dual	SC	1989
Chevron UK Ltd. (Alba Field)	North Sea	1	38000	Dual	HR	1991
KEG	UAE	2	76000	Dual	SC	1991
Power Company No. 2	Vietnam	3	114000	Dual	SC	1992
WED	Abu Dhabi	12	456000	Dual	SC	1992
National Power for SCA	England	1	38000	Dual	HR	1992
O.N.E.	Morocco	3	114000	Dual	SC	1993
IFV-Energi IS	Helsingor, Denmark	1	40000	Gas	CC	1993
PowerGen for Grovehurst Energy	England	1	38000	Gas	CC	1993
Sabah Electricity	Sabah	1	38000	Dual	SC	1994
Enemalta	Malta	2	76000	Dist	SC	1994
Pilbara Energy	Australia	3	114000	Dual	SC	1994
S.H.E. for Salt Union	England	1	38000	Dual	CC	1994
Pilbara Energy	Australia	2	76000	Dual	SC	1995
Y.P.F.	Argentina	2	76000	Gas	SC	1995
National Power/BASF	England	1	39160	Gas	CC	1995
Union Cement Company	UAE	1	39000	Gas	SC	1995
Hjorring Kommune	Denmark	1	39000	Gas	HR	1994
Kenya Power & Lighting	Kenya	1	37500	Dist	SC	1996
Sherritt Int. Power Corp.	Canada/Cuba	2	78000	Gas	SC*	1997
Kværner Construction for National Power/BASF	England	1	39000	Gas	CC	1997
Sherritt Int. Power Corp.	Canada/Cuba	1	38000	Gas	SC	1997
Sherritt Int. Power Corp.	Canada/Cuba	1	39000	Gas	SC*	1997
Genting Sanyen Power SND BHD	Malaysia	1	39000	Dual	SC	1997
ADCO, Asab	Abu Dhabi	2	78000	Gas	SC	1998
Sherritt Int. Power Corp.	Canada/Cuba	1	39000	Gas	HR	1999
Toyo Engineering Corp.	Thailand	1	39000	Gas	RP	1999
Total		**92**	**3468660**			

* later conversion to combined cycle

MS7001 Power Generation

Customer	Country	Number Ordered	Total Rating kW	Fuel	Cycle	Order Date
GE/Korea Electric Company	South Korea	1	65200	Dual	CC	1970
Sacramento Municipal Utility District	USA	1	78000	Dual	SC	1983
GE for Municipality of Anchorage	USA	1	78000	Dual	SC	1983
GE	USA	1	78000	Dist	SC	1983
Total		**4**	**299200**			

MS9001 Power Generation

Customer	Country	Number Ordered	Total Rating kW	Fuel	Cycle	Order Date
H.S.P.E/Dubai Aluminium	Dubai	5	437000	Dual	DS	1976
Ministry of Electricity & Water	Oman	3	324000	Dual	SC	1982
AEG for KHIC/Dubai Electricity Co.	Dubai	2	220000	Dual	DS	1986
TAVANIR	Iran	6	696000	Dual	SC	1989
North of Scotland Hydro Elec. Board	Scotland	2	232000	Gas	SC	1989
China Light & Power Co	Hong Kong	3	348000	Dist	SC	1990
SECWA	Australia	1	116000	Dual	SC	1990

MS9001   Power Generation (cont.)

Customer	Country	Number Ordered	Total Rating kW	Fuel	Cycle	Order Date
TAVANIR	Iran	14	1708000	Dual	SC	1991
SECWA	Australia	1	116000	Gas	SC	1991
Keadby Power Ltd	England	2	424000	Dual	CC	1992
TNB (Serdang)	Malaysia	2	246000	Dual	SC	1993
Minstry of Electricity & Water	Oman	2	246000	Dual	DS	1993
TNB (Pasir Gudang)	Malaysia	3	369000	Dual	SC	1993
Indian Queens	England	1	140000	Dist	SC	1995
Zhenhai Power Company	PRC	2	246000	Dist/HFO	CC	1996
Total		**49**	**5868000**			

Key
SC - Simple Cycle   CC - Combined Cycle   RC - Regenerative Cycle
HR - Heat Recovery   RP - Repowering   DS - Desalination

Bibliography and References

In the writing of this history, in addition to the specific titles listed below, a wide range of materials has been consulted, including: John Brown Engineering, Trafalgar House and Kvaerner company newsletters from 1966 to 2001, promotional literature, manuals, company and annual reports, several press cuttings collections pertaining primarily to John Brown Engineering and Trafalgar House, local and national newspapers, and periodicals dealing with the power engineering industry. In addition, John Brown Engineering's archives, Glasgow University's archives relating to shipbuilding, and General Electric's photographic archives have been consulted.

Anon (1951), *Clydebank Press*, 28 December.
Anon (1966), *The Times*, 26 July.
Anon (1967), *Clydebank Press*, 9 June, p11.
Anon (1971), "Increased potential for the heavy duty gas turbine in merchant ships: on board maintenance, study design, regenerative cycles and capacity for burning heavy oils are features of the heavy duty machine", reprinted from *The Motor Ship*, August.
Anon (1979), *Glasgow Herald*, 29 January.
Anon (1980), "Power in China Market", *Trafalgar House Group News*, No.3, January, p5.
Anon (1982), "JBE's quiet pace setter Graham R. Strachan CBE, Group Managing Director, John Brown Engineering", *World Energy News*, Spring, pp 10-11.
Anon (1982), "The Pipeline Allies in Disarray", *Time*, 2 August, No.31.
Anon (1985), "CHP is simply calorific", *Trafalgar House Today*, No.5, June, p12.
Anon (1987), *JBE will build and market uprated Mitsui SB60 design, Gas Turbine World*, March/April, (off print).
Anon (1993), "Keadby The World's first 9F Combined Cycle Power Plant designed, engineered and constructed by John Brown", reprinted from *Modern Power Systems*, September.
Anon (1993), "Three workers in Newark who didn't have to die", *People's Tribune*, January.
Anon (1994), "Kemsley Combined Heat and Power Plant designed, engineered and constructed by John Brown", reprinted from *Modern Power Systems*, September.
Anon (1995), "First combined heat and power plant for Oman", *John Brown Panorama*, August, pp20-21.
Anon (1995), "Power for the papermakers art", *John Brown Panorama*, March, pp28-29.
Anon (1995), "Tiger aids better turbine operation", *John Brown Panorama*, December, pp14-15.
Anon (1996), *Glasgow Herald*, 5 March.
Anon (2000), *Clydebank Post*, 23 November, p4.
Anon (2000), *Evening Times*, 16 November.
Anon (2000), *Evening Times*, December.
Anon (2000), *The Herald*, 23 December.
Anon (1996), "Indian Queens, Cornwall, UK: Synchronous Compensation and 140MW Peaking Plant", reprinted from *International Power Generation*, March.

Anon (1995), "Meeting the Cornish challenge", *Trafalgar House Today*, No.6, November, pp14-15.

Anon (n.d.), "Al Ghubrah, Sultanate of Oman 250 MW Combined Heat & Power Plant", reprinted from *International Power Generation*.

BP Petroleum Development Limited (n.d.), *The Miller Gas System*, (brochure).

Brown, H. (1953), *A History of the Clydebank establishment of Messrs. John Brown & Company (Clydebank) Limited, and of their predecessors James and George Thomson 1847-1953* (unpublished manuscript).

Brush Electrical Machines Limited (n.d.), *Installation List*.

Butcher, J.D. (1950), *Open and closed cycle gas turbines*, Transactions of Institution of Engineers and Shipbuilders in Scotland, January.

Chemical Age International (1979), July.

China Light & Power Company Limited (1972), *Hok Un Power Station*, (brochure).

Coats, R. and W. McDiarmid (n.d.), "Increased Efficiency and Output through Repowering".

Collective Agreements Negotiated with the Trade Unions which directly affect the Terms and Conditions of Employment, (n.d.), (booklet).

Connell, W. and A.J. Forsyth (1970), "Gas Turbine Power for the Emirate of Abu Dhabi: based on a paper presented at the General Electric Second European Gas Turbine State of the Art Congress, Palma de Mallorca", May, (off print).

Gray, T. (1991), "Serving the Water Industry", *John Brown Panorama*, Spring, pp22-23.

Hagen, Sturle (1996), "An Industrial Crusader", *Kværner Focus,* No.2, September, pp8-9.

JB News (1978), April.

JB News (1978), Winter.

JB News (1979), April/May.

JB News (1981), October.

JB Newsletter (1966), No.1, October.

JB Newsletter (1970), Autumn.

JB Newsletter (1970), Winter.

JB Newsletter (1971), Summer.

JB Newsletter (1972), Spring.

Jeffs, E. (1984), "JBE will maintain and operate Rusail Frame 9s", *Gas Turbine World*, September/October, pp20-21.

John Brown Engineering (1976), *JBE 10th Anniversary 1966-1976*, (leaflet).

John Brown Engineering (1988), "Gas Desulphurisation: An integrated contract capability from a single supplier", *Professional Engineering*, July.

John Brown Engineering (Clydebank) Limited (n.d.), *Marine Gas Turbine Propulsion Machinery*, (brochure).

John Brown Engineering Limited (n.d.), *ATP and the Chinese Power Station Contracts won by John Brown Engineering Limited in 1986: An analysis of UK benefits*, Clydebank: John Brown Engineering Limited.

John Brown Engineering Limited (n.d.), *Collective Agreements negotiated with the Trade Unions which directly affect the Terms and Conditions of Employment Hourly Paid*.

Johnston, I. (2000), *Ships for a Nation 1847-1971*, Dumbarton: West Dunbartonshire Libraries and Museums.

Kvaerner Energy (1988), *Gas Turbine Contracts Experience Summary*.

Kvaerner Focus (1996), No.1, July.

Kvaerner Focus (1998), November.

Law, B. (1990), "China Power Plant Commissioned", *John Brown Panorama*, Autumn, pp23-23.

McCabe, R.A. (1987), "John Brown: an export success story", Trafalgar Forum, Autumn, p13.

McKinstrey, S. (1997), "The Rise and Progress of John Brown Engineering, 1966-97: US Technology", *Scottish Enterprise and English Capital Business History*, Vol.39, No.3, pp105-34.

Mathers, N. (1990), "FGD cleans up for Power Gen", *John Brown Panorama*, November.

Mensforth, E. (1981), *Family Engineers*, London: Ward Lock Limited.

Nollen, S.D. (1986), "Business Costs and Business Policy for Export Controls", *Journal of International Business Studies*, Spring, p1-18.

North of Scotland Hydro-Electric Board (n.d.), *A Guide to Hydro-Electricity*, (brochure).

North of Scotland Hydro-Electric Board (n.d.), *Power from the Glens*, (brochure).

Payne, P.L. (1988), *The hydro: a study of the development of the major hydro-electric schemes undertaken by the North of Scotland Hydro-Electric Board*, Aberdeen: Aberdeen University Press.

PricewaterhouseCooper (1999), *Kvaerner Energy Thermal Power Information Memorandum*, July.

Shipbuilding Industry Committee (1966), *Shipbuilding Industry Committee 1965-66: Report*, March.

Strachan, G., *Unpublished and unfinished memoirs*.

Trafalgar House plc (1992), *Looking Towards the Future: A Report to Employees*.

Trafalgar House Today (1995), November.

Turner, J.A. (1981), *Metamorphosis*, Paper No.1437, Presidential Address [to] Institution of Engineers and Shipbuilders in Scotland, 6 October.